"Depressed? Anxious? Before you reach for a prescription, reach for *The Chemistry of Joy Workbook* and follow the instructions. This book is the answer and I highly recommend it!"

—Christiane Northrup, MD, ob/gyn physician and author of the *New York Times* bestsellers *Women's Bodies, Women's Wisdom* and *The Wisdom of Menopause*

"I have recommended Henry Emmons' *The Chemistry of Joy* to many people. In *The Chemistry of Joy Workbook*, he gives practical, actionable advice on boosting emotional resilience that is completely aligned with my own philosophy of integrative mental health. If you want to experience more positive moods, you will find this book most helpful."

—Andrew Weil, MD, author of *Spontaneous Happiness, Healthy Aging, Eight Weeks to Optimum Health*, and other books

"This book offers a brilliant new analysis of depression as a breakdown of positive mental and physical factors, and then gives readers a powerful toolbox of methods for restoring these factors in mind, heart, and body. Grounded in science, eminently practical, focused on the positive, and full of heart, this is a great resource for feeling better and for increasing the inner strength and resilience that will prevent depressed moods in the first place."

—Rick Hanson, PhD, author of *Buddha's Brain* and *Just One Thing*

"*The Chemistry of Joy Workbook* provides a wealth of practical information and advice for anyone who struggles with depression. Using readily available therapies and simple instructions, the expert authors offer a comprehensive self-care plan that addresses the causes of depression at the levels of body, mind, and spirit."

—James Lake, MD, chair of the International Network of Integrative Mental Health and author of the *Textbook of Integrative Mental Health Care*

"Many great wisdom traditions tell us that joy and happiness are not conditions that have to be created anew, but are natural and innate in everyone. Our task is to remove the obstructions that prevent us from realizing the inherent delight of life. *The Chemistry of Joy Workbook* is a marvelous tool that can help anyone accomplish this."

—Larry Dossey, MD, author of *The Power of Premonitions* and *Reinventing Medicine*

"*The Chemistry of Joy Workbook* gently, lovingly, and assuredly offers us the tools to reach the oasis of serenity we all seek, providing each of us with the opportunity to experience the best of what life has to offer."

—David Perlmutter, MD, FACN, ABIHM, author of *Power Up Your Brain*

"This is a workbook that actually works! It provides an excellent set of self-assessment tools that can help you better understand yourself and the causes of any psychological challenges you may be experiencing. It's practical and easy to understand, and it offers the opportunity for genuine insight."

—Phillip Moffitt, founder of the Life Balance Institute and author of *Emotional Chaos to Clarity* and *Dancing with Life*

"This workbook is a true lifeline. Follow its clear, engaging, expertly designed steps and you'll experience healing and thriving like never before."

—Raphael Cushnir, author of *The One Thing Holding You Back*

"A needed synthesis for people who need a balanced approach that incorporates the best wisdom of modern psychiatry and alternative medicine. This book communicates the science of brain chemistry in a straightforward manner, explaining the medical treatment of depression in plain English for the many people who want to understand the suffering inside them. I especially appreciate the compassion and the depth of experience that informs this useful book, from beginning to end. It is a work of great expertise and great love."

—Mary Hayes Grieco, director of The Midwest Institute for Forgiveness Training and author of *Unconditional Forgiveness*

"With extensive questionnaires, case examples, and individualized solutions covering all bases, this user-friendly workbook provides scientifically based recommendations for helping you reconnect with the joy that is your birthright. Just read and apply it—you will be happy you did!"

—Hyla Cass, MD, author of *Eight Weeks to Vibrant Health*

"Henry Emmons has done it again! A joyful way to take advantage of the healing he brings to us. What a great tool and a visionary message!"

—Kathleen DesMaisons, PhD, author of *Potatoes Not Prozac*

"This is a well-organized and clearly written book that shows a step-by-step process that enables the reader to create a richer and more meaningful internal life."

—Pia Mellody, author of *Facing Codependence* and *The Intimacy Factor*

"If there were one book I could give to every person who wants to love the life they are living and live the life they love, it would be this one. It is fertilizer for the life force that is your birthright."

—Dawna Markova, PhD, author of *I Will Not Die an Unlived Life*, *Wide Open*, and coeditor of *Random Acts of Kindness*

"This book is an outstanding example of the emerging field of the mind-body-diet connection. It represents a clinically validated pathway to increased happiness that translates into a greater joy of life."

—Barry Sears, PhD, author of *The Zone*

"*The Chemistry of Joy* has helped many people who suffer from depression not only survive, but thrive. This workbook will multiply those numbers as it leads the reader through a series of reflective exercises and practices that flow from the notion that personal change comes from self-acceptance. In true Henry Emmons style, the approach is well-grounded and serious but appropriately lighthearted—exactly what's needed by people who are weighed down with self-reproach. In the words of a Buddhist teacher whose spirit reminds me of Emmons', 'You are perfect as you are—and you could use a little improvement!'"

—Parker J. Palmer, author of *Healing the Heart of Democracy*, *Let Your Life Speak*, and *The Courage to Teach*

"This workbook mirrors Emmons himself in many ways: it is kind, insightful, supportive, practical, and wise. Here is a fabulous tool for those struggling with depression. The authors have created the best guide available to become happier and more resilient."

—Scott Shannon, MD, psychiatrist and assistant clinical professor in the department of psychiatry at the University of Colorado

"*The Chemistry of Joy Workbook* is not just another self-help workbook. Henry Emmons, Susan Bourgerie, Carolyn Denton, and Sandra Kacher have created a remarkable roadmap to rediscovering our innate potential for flourishing, optimum health. They remind us that the next revolution in healthcare does not lie in the discovery of more medical magic bullets but in supporting our potential for resilience. This workbook will be an invaluable resource for my patients and for me. I look forward to walking the pathways to health with them."

—James Duffy, MD, FANPA, psychiatrist and chief of integrative medicine
at Sierra Tucson

"Blending the wisdom of traditional healing approaches with the rigor of scientific strategies, *The Chemistry of Joy Workbook* is filled with insightful ideas and empowering practices that will not only help to heal the despair and isolation of individuals with depression, but will serve as a guide to personal growth and transformation at the heart of living a life of meaning, connection, and well-being. Soak in these healing suggestions and give yourself the beginnings of a new way of life."

—Daniel J. Siegel, MD, executive director of the Mindsight Institute and clinical professor
at the University of California, Los Angeles School of Medicine

"As I read through *The Chemistry of Joy Workbook*, the word heuristic repeatedly came to mind. A 'heuristic' is an experience-based technique for problem solving, learning, and discovery. Henry Emmons and team have written a book rich in heuristic-like solutions to an eternal dilemma: Why are we unhappy and how does this lack of joy further complicate our lives? Step by step, and through a brilliant journal-like design, *The Chemistry of Joy Workbook* identifies and unravels the obstacles to the science of satisfaction."

—Peter D'Adamo, ND, MIFHI, author of *Eat Right 4 Your Type* and director, Center
of Excellence in Generative Medicine, University of Bridgeport

"A thoughtful, user-friendly, wide-ranging guide to attitudes and practices that will make your journey through depression easier, faster, and more fruitful."

—James S. Gordon, MD, founder and director of The Center for Mind Body Medicine
and author of *Unstuck: Your Guide to the Seven-Stage Journey Out of Depression*

The Chemistry of Joy Workbook

OVERCOMING DEPRESSION USING
THE BEST OF BRAIN SCIENCE, NUTRITION, AND
THE PSYCHOLOGY OF MINDFULNESS

HENRY EMMONS, MD, SUSAN BOURGERIE, MA, LP,
CAROLYN DENTON, MA, LN, and SANDRA KACHER, MSW, LICSW

New Harbinger Publications, Inc.

Distributed in Canada by Raincoast Books

Copyright © 2012 by Henry Emmons
New Harbinger Publications, Inc.
5674 Shattuck Avenue
Oakland, CA 94609
www.newharbinger.com

All Rights Reserved
Acquired by Jess O'Brien; Cover design by Amy Shoup; Edited by Rosalie Wieder

Library of Congress Cataloging-in-Publication Data

Printed in the United States of America

14 13 12

10 9 8 7 6 5 4 3 2 1   First printing

Contents

Part 3
The Mind Pathways

Part 4
The Heart Pathways

Introduction

Restoring the Elements of a Resilient Life

Surely joy is the condition of life.

Henry David Thoreau

Resilience is natural. Even after a long, hard winter, when the proper conditions arrive, nature simply springs back to life of its own accord.

Resilience may be natural, yet every day we encounter people who are enduring a hard inner winter, whose joy and vitality have long ago gone dormant. Many of them have lost heart. Having tried all the usual remedies with little success, they wonder if they will ever fully reclaim their lives. They come to us with a single question, framed in a thousand different ways: "What can I do to feel better, to bring myself back to life, to recover the joy that I have lost?"

This workbook is our answer to that question, and we are so glad to share it with you. We are a team of healers trained in holistic psychiatry, integrative nutrition, and the psychology of mindfulness. We have a shared passion for blending the elements from these different ways of knowing into a coherent, healing whole. Our goal is simple: to offer insights, strategies, and skills that really work.

How do we know that this approach works?

- It is based upon the most current research in neuroscience, genetic expression, nutrition, and the psychological sciences.

- The inner skills we offer come from the wisdom of mindfulness, which has been a powerful antidote to human suffering for over 2,500 years.

- We have witnessed thousands of people reclaim their lives from depression, anxiety, and other stress-related conditions by following the pathways that we will describe in this book.

- We practice these skills ourselves and we know firsthand how life giving they can be.

THE ENEMIES OF JOY

Though it is often hard to see life as essentially joyful, we believe that it is. While it may be hidden, the experience of joy is natural and effortless, and it is available to us at all times, whether or not we are aware of its presence.

A man approached one of us after a workshop to say how much he appreciated this truth. "My son died two years ago," he explained, "and I was devastated. I sank into a dark depression. Your work helped me to reconnect to the joy that was his short life. Now I can carry sorrow and joy at the same time, and the one no longer outweighs the other."

This man knows that joy is not merely a feeling; it does not mean that we are always happy or expansive. Sadness, loss, and sorrow are not the opposite of joy, and they do not necessarily prevent us from accessing it. Joy involves an accepting stance toward life, a deep connection with that which is most life giving, a sense of gratitude that arises spontaneously when we realize the abundance that is in our lives.

Joy comes of its own accord when we are in our naturally healthy state. Yet it requires that we be resilient, and there are many forces that sabotage our efforts to remain resilient and so block our access to joy. These enemies of joy result in:

- an imbalanced body

- an unsettled mind

- a disconnected heart

All are signs that our resilience is under siege.

In each of these categories, there are outside forces beyond our personal control, but also things we do to ourselves that unwittingly cause us more harm:

- The imbalanced body is assaulted from the outside by exposure to toxins, such as pollution, food additives, radiation, and other harmful forms of energy—and from the inside by our own diet and lifestyle choices.

- The unsettled mind is accosted from the outside by stresses such as emotional or physical trauma, the weight of others' expectations, disturbing images or news items, financial uncertainty, or personal loss—and from the inside by the attachments of our own minds.

- The disconnected heart is burdened from the outside by the experience of loneliness or isolation caused by social upheaval, loss of loved ones, ruptures in relationships—and from the inside by our own tendency to shut down and withdraw whenever we feel threatened.

Even the most resilient among us may become fearful or depressed when visited by several of these enemies at once. And even those who are most vulnerable may remain resilient if they take care to keep restoring themselves in the face of that which is depleting.

This workbook is designed to guide you toward balancing your body, settling your mind, and connecting your heart, so that the enemies of joy have far less power over you. They can be fierce, but you can be just as fierce in how you respond to them.

THE BREAKDOWN OF RESILIENCE

Resilience is essential to the joyful life. When you have a deep source of resilience and the skills to maintain it, you are able to adapt to change, to face challenges, and to deal with life's inevitable stresses and still come out all right, perhaps even strengthened, on the other end. In this naturally resilient state, joy can enter of its own accord, just as the grass grows in springtime simply because the conditions for its growth have returned.

Resilience is your nature, yet it is under siege. Mental and emotional disorders are now epidemic, creating great personal and societal suffering:

- Of Americans over age eighteen, 26.2 percent (more than one in four adults in this country) suffer from some type of diagnosable mental disorder in any given year (Kessler et al. 2005), and nearly half of them meet criteria for more than one disorder (U.S. Census Bureau 2005).

- Mood disorders, including major depression, *dysthymia* (a milder but chronic depression), and bipolar disorder, affect 20 million Americans (10 percent) each year (Kessler et al. 2005). Depression is the leading cause of disability in the United States, and will soon be number one throughout the world (World Health Organization 2008).

- According to IMS Health, as reported by National Public Radio (Shute 2011), doctors wrote 254 million prescriptions for antidepressant drugs in 2010, making them the second most prescribed drugs after cholesterol-lowering medications.

- Anxiety is even more common, with one in five (60 million) people in the United States suffering from a diagnosable anxiety disorder (Kessler et al. 2005).

There are a host of other conditions that are also stress related, such as insomnia, hypertension, heart disease, memory disorders, gastrointestinal problems, and drug and alcohol abuse. Virtually every chronic illness is impacted by stress.

The frequency of these problems has increased dramatically over the past few decades. What can be done to reverse this breakdown in resilience?

RESILIENCE IS NOT LOST, JUST WAITING TO BE REAWAKENED

We have worked with thousands of people, individually and in groups, to help them reclaim their lives from the grip of depression. Surely, this takes courage, and courage is aided by the belief that it is at least *possible*—not only for others, but also for you—to awaken to joy. What has worked for thousands of others can also work for you.

If you were in our offices, you would hear stories of inspiration like these:

Cheryl has a rich life with a rewarding career, three lovely children, and a supportive husband and friends. There seemed to be no reason for it, yet she had suffered frequent and debilitating depressive episodes throughout her life, despite very good mental health care. In the spring following her participation in our program, she said, "For the first time in my adult life, I made it through the winter without a depressive episode!" That was four years ago, and she still remains healthy, vibrant, and active. Her depression has not returned.

William, who had had unremitting depression since his teenage years, said, "Although I didn't find the 'magic cure' I'd been looking for, I now accept myself—depression and all—and feel more hope than I ever have before." He felt hopeful because now he was learning that there were choices he could make and things he could do for himself that clearly improved his mood. He had a sense of direction and a set of skills that he finally believed offered a way out of lifelong depression.

Allison not only recovered from a severe depression, she also went further: "It made it seem possible to move from depression to actual joy, not just to a place free from pain."

Individuals are able to reclaim more of their lives, because this is an approach that integrates many aspects of what it takes to live a resilient and joyful life. We are addressing the sources of suffering from several angles and bolstering the skills of resilience through multiple avenues.

One of our integrative programs is called Resilience Training. Our research with this program shows that nearly everyone who follows it improves, and most recover fully, even from the severe form of this illness known as major depression (Dusek et al. 2009). Here are some of the highlights from our research:

- Depression scores dropped by 71 percent.

- Over 60 percent of participants achieved full remission from depression.

- There was a 71 percent improvement in quality-of-life measures.

- Similar improvements were found in perceived stress, anxiety, and work productivity.

Our goal is for you, too, to find relief from suffering, whatever is causing it and however it appears in your life. We want you to reclaim your birthright gift of resilience and the joy that accompanies it.

Resilience is a renewable resource that depends more on skill than on genetics, circumstances, or sheer luck. This book is devoted to helping you restore and maintain that resource so that joy can flow back into your life.

Part 1

Preparing for the Journey

Chapter 1

Pathways to Joy:

Make This Journey Your Own

Caminante, no hay camino, se hace camino al andar.
[Traveler, there is no path. You make the path by walking.]

Antonio Machado

Restoring the elements of a resilient life requires that we each make our own path. It begins with a single step, but that alone will not make it a path. That first step must be followed by another and then again by another.

When your resilience is depleted, it may seem an overwhelming prospect to take even that first step. There is a tendency to blame yourself for an inability to "snap out of it," yet most people have no real guidance on how to reclaim their lives.

The aim of this workbook is to give you that guidance and to help you create and follow your own path to a resilient and joyful life. Each person's path is unique, yet there are a few elements that form the essence of the journey for all of us. We offer nine such elements, *pathways* that can restore your resilience and open you to at least the possibility of a joyful life.

THE PATHWAYS TO JOY

There is no single "key" to happiness or success. People cannot be reduced to a few brain chemicals, or to certain repetitive thoughts or negative beliefs, or even to a diminished spirit. The real power in this program lies in its being a unified approach that embraces different facets of what it means to be fully human. It is a true integration of the various elements of resilience, blended into a coherent whole.

The following nine pathways will help you reclaim your resilience and your capacity for joy. They are grouped into three clusters, representing different aspects of who we are as human beings: body, mind, and heart. They provide powerful antidotes to the enemies of joy that were described briefly in the introduction: an imbalanced body, an unsettled mind, and a disconnected heart.

The Body Pathways

Caring for the body provides you with the conditions to thrive. By themselves, these pathways will not guarantee joyfulness or resilience. Yet they are essential for a resilient life. The three body pathways—nurturing, balancing, and flowing—will help you to establish a solid foundation for resilience so that the rest of your journey can be deeply fruitful.

THE FIRST PATHWAY

nurturing

In the first pathway, we examine how the information your body derives from food influences its functioning. You will identify any missing ingredients—or systems that may be out of balance—that prevent your body from naturally self-correcting. Questionnaires will help you discover if there are physical areas that you need to address, and if so, we offer specific guidance on how to do so.

THE SECOND PATHWAY

balancing

A healthy mood can only be sustained if brain chemistry is balanced in the best way for your individual needs. What is called "depression" is not just one thing that can be treated in the same way for each person. This second pathway helps you determine whether you may have a specific type of brain-chemical imbalance. We will then help you create your own plan for optimal nutritional supplementation so that your hard-won natural balance can last.

THE THIRD PATHWAY

flowing

This pathway reminds us that we are part of the natural world and aligning with it is a key to resilience. There are natural cycles that impact mood, including daily rhythms, sleep, and seasons. Yet each of us has our own unique lifestyle patterns and needs. Our questionnaire helps you discover your mind-body type, and we provide information that helps you design a practical and effective plan to flow more easily with your own nature.

The Mind Pathways

One foundation of our approach is the good medicine of mindfulness, grounded in 2,600 years of Eastern wisdom. A mindful life can lead to a calm and joyful mind. By following the three pathways of settling, opening, and knowing, you will help the mind to become calmer, to open to your experience, and to see more clearly so that you will be able to face whatever arises in your life with greater wisdom and equanimity.

THE FOURTH PATHWAY

settling

The untamed mind easily jumps from thought to thought without awareness or intention. Its activity is unceasing, and it seems powerfully drawn to harmful thoughts and painful emotions. The good news is that, like an impulsive puppy, the mind can learn to quiet, indeed to "Sit!" In the fourth pathway, we introduce you to the basics of mindfulness practice, which will enable the mind to settle and the body to relax.

THE FIFTH PATHWAY

opening

Learning to fully experience the complete range of human emotions is a fundamental part of recovery from depression and of creating a joyful life. In this chapter you can learn to turn toward even painful emotions, grounded in mindful awareness of their impermanence and your capacity to feel them without being overwhelmed. And you'll discover the truth that being emotionally aware leads you to discover life's joys in a deeper way.

THE SIXTH PATHWAY

knowing

Grounded in mindfulness, you will gain perspective on some of your most intensely painful emotional experiences and learn more skillful ways of responding to them in the moment. These experiences offer you the chance to develop greater self-awareness and a sense of mastery. The tools you will learn in this chapter can dramatically improve your sense of well-being and help prevent the recurrence of depression.

The Heart Pathways

There is much that happens beneath the surface of awareness in every person's inner life. You can lay the groundwork of good physical health, tame your wild mind, and expand your capacity to be with the full range of emotions. But without connection to the larger world, including the unseen mysteries, you lose touch with your deepest and most life-sustaining energies. Your taproots need to sink deeply into this life source in order to thrive, and that involves connection with the inner self, with others, and with spiritual truths and practices. Following the pathways of connecting, belonging, and deepening gives access to these deeper sources to nourish resilience and create the conditions for lasting joy.

THE SEVENTH PATHWAY

connecting

One of the most disheartening aspects of depression is the sense of separation, isolation, and shame that so often comes with it. Moving out of this isolation begins with authentic acceptance of and connection with yourself.

In the seventh pathway, we challenge the illusion that you are isolated and defective, and guide you toward wholeness and connection with your basic goodness. We offer meditations and exercises that work to heal disconnection from self and transform your capacity for love of self and others.

THE EIGHTH PATHWAY

belonging

In the eighth pathway, we move further into the healing power of connection and explore the possibilities of creating a genuine sense of belonging and community.

Transformation begins within. We offer powerful meditation practices that help you move beyond yourself to find joy in interconnection with others and the larger world. We follow this inner work with recommendations for actions that help you create a place of belonging for yourself.

THE NINTH PATHWAY

deepening

One of the most disheartening enemies of joy is disconnection from your deepest, most authentic self. The deepening path outlined in this final pathway leads you to an opportunity to reclaim your own inner wisdom. We draw from depth spirituality and our own experience to make listening to the voice within both accessible and meaningful.

HOW TO USE THIS WORKBOOK

The pathways to joy are integrated, with each one supporting the next. We suggest that you begin by rebalancing the body, then settling the mind, and finally connecting with heart. Yet the pathways are also fluid and interconnected, so they can be done in any way that best suits your needs. You may find that a particular set of pathways is especially important for you. Or you may wish to revisit a pathway that you have strayed from in order to strengthen it. The following are examples of how you can make this program your own.

- ## Clare's Story: A Focus on Body

Clare was a fifty-two-year-old woman who had experienced mild to moderate depression most of her life. While there were periods when she had felt strong and resilient, the past several months had become especially difficult for her. She had other lifelong health issues, such as migraine headaches, frequent sinus infections, and dermatitis. She was frustrated with herself because she has an insatiable sweet tooth and had gained weight during the past year. She had recently found out that she was vitamin D deficient. She also felt fatigued due to poor sleep, which made it hard for her to concentrate. After completing the resilience skills questionnaire, Clare found that working toward rebalancing her body would be most important to her overall success in this program.

- ## Paula's Story: A Focus on Mind

Paula felt as if she had been swimming in stress hormones since childhood. Her parents were emotionally abusive and had very high expectations for her success. Paula eventually became CEO of a large company and held the job for twenty-five years. She had recently retired and moved back to her hometown to be near family. Until the move, life had been full and fast paced. Then, despite the diminishing of her outward stress, she became unable to sleep and her mind was unfocused. "I feel like I'm living outside of myself," she said. Her score on the resilience skills questionnaire suggested that she put special emphasis on settling her mind.

• *Frank's Story: A Focus on Heart*

At the age of forty, Frank had been struggling with self-acceptance for thirteen years, starting shortly after he came out to his family as gay. He was very hard on himself and tended to be a perfectionist. Recently transferred to a new city for his job, he became socially isolated. He was still able to function at work, but he started sleeping excessively and not eating regularly. He was beginning to feel as if he was not worthy of being loved. Frank's scores on the resilience skills questionnaire helped him decide to put most of his energy into strengthening his connection with heart.

SO HOW SHOULD YOU BEGIN?

Each step in the program is meant to build upon all of the previous ones. It always works well to start at the beginning and follow them in order, but we encourage you to make this process your own by focusing on the pathways most important to you. The following resilience skills questionnaire will help guide you in deciding where to begin. You will discover what you are already doing well but will also see where your resilience skills risk becoming depleted. Your results will help you decide where to place your attention and energy so that you can recover your own access to joy.

Remember that these are skills you naturally possess, but they need to be refreshed and renewed throughout your life, especially if you have encountered numerous enemies of joy along the way.

Resilience Skills Questionnaire

For each question below, circle the number that is most true for you:

1—Hardly ever

2—Some of the time

3—As often as not

4—Most of the time

5—Nearly always

1. I take time to provide and prepare nourishing foods, and I eat with enjoyment and awareness. 1 2 3 4 5

2. I notice when I am hungry or when I am full, and I act accordingly. 1 2 3 4 5

3. I am aware of the signals my body gives me when I am under too much stress. 1 2 3 4 5

Nurturing Score (chapter 3)—add scores for questions 1–3: _____

4. I bounce back fairly quickly from low moods. 1 2 3 4 5

5. I supplement my diet with key nutritional products specific for my body. 1 2 3 4 5

6. I recognize the pattern of my down moods and support myself with effective natural or prescription therapies when needed. 1 2 3 4 5

Balancing Score (chapter 4)—add scores for questions 4–6: _____

7. When I feel depleted, I know what I can do to restore my energy. 1 2 3 4 5

8. I enjoy moving my body, and I intentionally do some kind of movement every day. 1 2 3 4 5

9. I seldom feel rushed, and I slow down or rest when I need to. 1 2 3 4 5

Flowing Score (chapter 5)—add scores for questions 7–9: _____

10. I try to do one thing at a time and pay attention to what I am doing in the here and now. 1 2 3 4 5

11. I can sense when my thoughts are rushing, and I pause to calm my mind. 1 2 3 4 5

12. I can accept my thoughts without judgment. 1 2 3 4 5

Settling Score (chapter 6)—add scores for questions 10–12: _____

13. I am open to the whole range of my emotions and am comfortable feeling them. 1 2 3 4 5

14. I realize that all emotional experiences are impermanent, that none last forever. 1 2 3 4 5

15. I am aware of my emotions as I feel them in my body, and don't get caught up in overthinking them. 1 2 3 4 5

Opening Score (chapter 7)—add scores for questions 13–15: _____

16. I can see that my thoughts are not my reality, and I am able to let them go before they have much impact on my mood. 1 2 3 4 5

17. I know what kinds of situations are likely to trigger a flood of negative feelings in me. 1 2 3 4 5

18. When an overwhelmingly bad mood hits me, I know how to work with it to minimize the trouble it creates for me. 1 2 3 4 5

Knowing Score (chapter 8)—add scores for questions 16–18: _____

19. I like and accept myself as I am, even if I could use some improvement. 1 2 3 4 5

20. I am easily moved when I see someone else suffering, and my heart opens to him or her. 1 2 3 4 5

21. I treat others and myself with kindness. 1 2 3 4 5

Connecting Score (chapter 9)—add scores for questions 19–21: _____

22. I feel comforted in knowing how many people support and care for me. 1 2 3 4 5

23. I have people in my life to whom I can go with matters of the heart. 1 2 3 4 5

24. I feel part of ever-larger circles, including family, friends, local community, tribe, nation, and world community. 1 2 3 4 5

Belonging Score (chapter 10)—add scores for questions 22–24: _____

25. I pause during the day for reflection, or to take time to center myself. 1 2 3 4 5

26. I am satisfied with my spiritual practice. 1 2 3 4 5

27. I usually listen to and heed my inner voice. 1 2 3 4 5

Deepening Score (chapter 11)—add scores for questions 25–27: _____

Scoring:

- Add together the numbers you circled within each of the nine subgroups. Add all the subgroup scores to get your overall resilience skills score: _____ .

- A score of 108–135 means that you have kept your resilience skills in good shape and that is likely to pay off in giving you a sense of well-being or joy. Use your subgroup scores to determine where to put your energy to assure that you will stay healthy and happy.

- A score of 81–107 means that your resilience skills are still moderately strong but not at their peak and this may put your mood at risk. Use your subgroup scores to help you choose those areas most likely to raise your resilience skills back to a high level and prevent stress-related problems.

- A score of 54–80 means that your resilience skills are low and you are at high risk, or may already have symptoms of depression, anxiety, or another stress-related condition. Your subgroup scores will tell you where you are most depleted and where to put most of your energy, but you should follow all parts of the resilience pathway to get yourself back on track.

The Chemistry of Joy Workbook

- A score of 27–53 means that your resilience skills are depleted, and you very likely have symptoms of depression, anxiety, or both. Remember that these skills can be reclaimed; they are just waiting for you to begin building them back up by following all the steps along the pathway to resilience.

Next, place your subgroup scores in the table below. They correspond to the nine pathways to joy. By comparing your scores across the pathways, you can decide where to begin and where to put most of your effort.

	SUBGROUP	YOUR SUBGROUP SCORE	PATHWAY
The Body Pathways	1		*Nurturing: Care for Your Body* (chapter 3)
	2		*Balancing: Support Your Brain* (chapter 4)
	3		*Flowing: Live in Rhythm with Your Nature* (chapter 5)
The Mind Pathways	4		*Settling: Take the Mindful Path to a Calm Mind* (chapter 6)
	5		*Opening: Develop Emotional Resilience* (chapter 7)
	6		*Knowing: Become a Source of Wisdom for Yourself* (chapter 8)
The Heart Pathways	7		*Connecting: Come Home to Yourself* (chapter 9)
	8		*Belonging: Create Circles of Connection* (chapter 10)
	9		*Deepening: Renew Yourself from Within* (chapter 11)

- 13–15: This resilience skill is strong. Keep up the good work and look to see if another area is more in need of your attention.

- 10–12: While still moderately strong, this skill is beginning to weaken. If you act to shore it up now, you may prevent future problems.

- 7–9: This skill is fading, placing you at risk. Be sure to address it quickly within the program.

- 3–6: This skill has eroded. You can still reclaim it by beginning right away with the corresponding pathway. Doing the entire program will ensure that you are doing all you can to rebuild your resilience.

Additional Support

Throughout this workbook you will find meditations, guided imagery, and other exercises that will become more effective the more you practice them. The written instructions will provide everything you need to do the practices, but you may find it helpful to be guided through them by an audio version of the instructions. If you would like to receive additional support in this way, go to www.partnersin resilience.com, where you can download the practices and also find recorded talks, courses, and links to other resources.

SUMMING UP CHAPTER 1

- The pathways to joy are intended to be fluid and integrated, each one connecting and supporting the next, interrelated and interdependent.

- The journey is flexible and can be adapted to your own needs. You can focus your energy on the skills most in need of your attention and revisit any paths that you have strayed from in order to strengthen them.

- The nine pathways to joy are a lifelong pursuit, sure to enhance resilience and open the door to joy.

Chapter 2

Beginning:

Tap into Your Source

Nobody can go back and start a new beginning,
but anyone can start today and make a new ending.

Maria Robinson

Y ou may have doubts about how much you can change your life to become more joyful. You may think that it's possible for others but not for you. Perhaps your earlier attempts to create a new beginning have brought you to the same old stuck place. Perhaps it's even been too difficult to attempt a new start. We want to assure you that you *can* make a new life and that you can start today.

The change process that you will learn engages your whole self. That's because this program is built upon a synergistic combination of changes in body, mind, and heart, a process that honors all of who you are as a complex human being. This whole-person approach can work for you even if others have not.

THE WHOLE-PERSON CHANGE PROCESS

Whole-person change is a deep change process with several principles at its core.

Whole-person change is grounded in radical self-acceptance. This is not simply another self-improvement project. The starting point is acceptance of yourself and your life just as they are at this moment in time. This runs counter to the usual approach, which is rooted in self-criticism and the drive for "a better me." We're not talking about a passive or resigned state of acceptance, but one that is energized and forward looking. *Arugamama* is a Japanese word that captures this dynamic tension. It is a state of unconditional acceptance of yourself and your life as they are at this moment, but with the simultaneous intention to act in positive ways to create change. As the Buddhist teacher Suzuki-roshi humorously put it, "Each of you is perfect the way you are…and you could use a little improvement!" (Chadwick 2007, 1). Beginning with this energized self-acceptance is the ultimate "start where you are" stance.

Whole-person change begins deep within. The most sustaining motivation for change comes from connecting mindfully and compassionately with your inner suffering and the desire for relief from that suffering. Change that is based on what you believe you should be, or based on the standards set by others, is often short-lived. Being willing to listen deeply and honor your desire for change in a compassionate way leads to sustainable change.

Whole-person change embraces even resistance to change. Most of us become frustrated when we can't seem to make life changes that we know are good for us. Yet resistance to change is natural. Rather than wishing it away, we must accept that resistance is there, look more deeply into its nature, and learn to work with it more skillfully.

All change is a process, and not a linear one. The self-improvement model of change often gives the impression that, if you are doing it right, you will experience continuous and sequential improvement. In the whole-person change process, you may go on and off the path of change many times, and may even feel as if you're going back to the beginning. That is normal and expected. You only need to acknowledge it, pick yourself up wherever you are, and return to the pathway you have set upon. There's an old Japanese proverb that says it simply: "Fall down seven times, get up eight." The important thing is to notice when you've fallen and get back on the path.

Change happens in connection. In contrast to our individualistic Western culture, which puts the onus on the individual to initiate and accomplish change, we believe it is important to reach beyond yourself in the healing process—to build your network of connection that will feed and sustain you as you change. This network will include family, friends, and community, as well as connection with your own spirit and a source of meaning and purpose in your life.

THE SELF-IMPROVEMENT MODEL OF CHANGE

Like all human beings, you have made many life changes—some more successful than others. Let's take a look at a very common approach to change and see if you recognize any of your own change efforts. This approach is rooted in the strong drive for self-improvement and is fueled by a sense of self-deficiency.

It is common to identify with the *inner critic*, who, unfortunately, believes that criticism, disapproval, and harshness are *required* in order to create change. It is the critic that drives self-improvement projects. The example below describes Sandy's desired change—"to get in shape"—and the driving thoughts and actions as well as the types of outcomes that resulted from this self-critical approach.

Sandy's Desire	Driving Thoughts and Actions	Sandy's Outcomes
To get in shape fast	*You are so fat! I can't stand how you look! The only way you're going to get anywhere is to do something drastic!* In an effort to get into shape quickly, Sandy signed up for a yoga boot-camp weekend. She spent two days stretching every muscle in her body, pushing those stretches way beyond comfort, and holding the stretches for far too long.	• Ten days encased in the armor of rigid muscles • A day of missed work because it hurt too much to move • Foolish pride in her capacity for self-punishment • A deep need for comfort that she tried to satisfy with a giant bag of Cheetos

The primary problem with this approach is that it just doesn't work; it keeps the cycle of self-criticism going, and you end up feeling even worse about yourself for failing yet again. In contrast to the critic-based self-improvement model, the whole-person model of change begins from a position of self-acceptance.

THE SELF-ACCEPTANCE MODEL OF CHANGE

The poet Walt Whitman wrote: "I am larger, better than I thought; I did not know I held so much goodness" (Whitman 2004).

We share the poet's belief that you are larger than you imagine yourself to be. It is when you value and engage all of yourself that you can begin to create the lasting changes that you long for.

Let's look at an example of such an approach to change. Like Sandy, Martha felt she was out of shape. She often felt stiff and sluggish. She wanted to have more energy and feel more at home in her body. But she went about changing herself in a far more accepting way.

Martha's Desire	Self-Accepting Thoughts and the Actions That Follow	Outcomes
To get in shape, feel more energetic, and feel more at home in her body	*I accept my body as it is at this moment and long for something better.* *I can start where I am and build slowly toward my goals.* *I know if I push myself too hard, I will rebel.* She enrolled in a beginner's yoga class at a small, friendly studio within walking distance of her home. Because it was easy to get to and the class was welcoming, she completed the first session and signed up for another.	• She felt more flexible. • She began to look forward to the classes. • She made some yoga friends who supported her change. • She felt more empowered to make changes in other parts of her life.

As you work through this process, you will learn to not only change your behaviors but also expand your view of yourself and your capacity for change.

FROM CRITIC TO VISIONARY

Too often the loudest inner voice is that of the small self with its tone of self-criticism. We need to diminish that voice in favor of one that has a larger vision for our lives. We need to silence the inner critic and listen to the inner visionary.

The Critic

The critic whispers incessantly to you about your shortcomings, about all that is wrong and how hard you must work to change. Most of us have a list that includes such things as "sad," "angry," "lazy," "fat," "out of shape," "selfish," and so on. What's on your list?

_____

_____

The critic creates the belief that you must strive for perfection and hide what is imperfect. But there is another part of you that we'd like to introduce right now, and we offer this part as a companion to the critic. This part is the visionary.

The Visionary

The visionary knows who you really are, identifies with your basic goodness, and has specific longings just for you. The visionary does not demand perfection or compare you to others who are better, smarter, more motivated, or more of anything than you are. The visionary is a bridge to your potential. When the visionary is engaged, you experience more energy and more endurance. As the critic is motivated by fear of who you will be if you don't get it right, the visionary is motivated by love of who you want to be—and are.

The Vision Board: Connecting with Your Visionary

An excellent way to work with your visionary is to create a vision board. Making a vision board is an activity that engages your longings, your intuitions, and your spontaneity. Once you've gathered the necessary materials, it will take you about an hour to create your board.

1. The materials you will need include poster board, scissors, glue stick or tape, markers, and a stack of magazines with lots of pictures. Set these items out around you and think back to the moment you decided to buy this workbook. Where were you? What about it called to you? What hopes did it stir for you? What hopes do you have now for yourself in going through this workbook? Jot them down here.

_____

_____

_____

2. Something vital lives under the weariness and discouragement of depression. However distant you may sometimes feel from this vitality, it hasn't left you. Access your wish to live from this place and, holding on to this connection as much as you can, take a ramble through your magazines. Cut or tear out any words or images that capture your attention—no questions asked!

When you have a substantial supply of materials, play with placing them on your poster board. Don't worry about placing them just right; with this project there is no wrong.

3. After you've completed your own vision board, sit with it, admire it, enjoy it. And then begin to harvest its message; write down in a few words or sentences what it tells you about your intentions for yourself on this journey.

    Here is an example: The sunlight tells me how much I want to get away from the darkness I feel, the balloons suggest buoyancy, the travel pictures tell me how much I want to get away from the sameness of my life, and the running shoes show me that it's time to get moving!

    What does your vision board tell you about your deepest longings and intentions for yourself on this journey to resilience?

---

4. Finally, see if you can crystallize, in a sentence or two, what your intentions are for yourself as you go through this workbook. The more you know your intentions, the clearer will be your purpose and the sturdier it will be in providing you support.

    Sample intention statements: I am going to learn how to support and increase my physical energy. I want to experience more support in my life. I intend to listen less to the critic and more to the visionary.

FROM VISION TO ACTION

The process of moving from vision to action is not linear. If you buy into the belief that you can set a goal and never waver from implementing it, the journey is likely to fail. It can fail not because you lack the will or have a weak character, but because aspects of the human brain make change challenging and incremental. Lasting change is almost always a process of movement and activity alternating with rest and consolidation.

There is a strong paradox in the change process. You may think it should be easy to make positive, healthy changes in your life, yet your own biology can make it difficult. Our brains are wired to keep things as they are:

- Thoughts are strengthened with every repetition. This makes it easy to have a thought again and yet again, to the point that thoughts can become automatic.

- Anything that can be delegated to unconscious processes will be. This doesn't refer just to things like oxygenating your blood but also to daily habits. How many times have you driven to work only to realize you don't remember three-quarters of the trip?

- Brain activity is altered by the perception that you are under threat. Change can feel threatening, making it harder to think clearly. Attention is more drawn to threat than to possibility. Hope about the future takes a backseat to survival.

The brain's very structure supports its tendency to conserve the old. Conscious change is difficult because the brain is wired to preserve things as they are, including our thinking and feeling habits. And yet the human brain is full of innovation. Throughout this workbook we will give you strategies to work with this tendency more skillfully.

The 51 Percent Solution

When you bump up against the tendency to stay in old ruts, you experience what is known as "resistance." You might think that some part of you is willfully sabotaging your desire to change. We prefer to refer to this as "habit energy." This reminds us that doing the same thing over and over again is inherently reinforcing. Sometimes people say such things as, "I must be getting something out of it or I wouldn't keep doing it." In these words they hear the voice of the critic. The visionary might be more inclined to say, "I know that I am capable of change, but let's take a realistic look at what it might take." The visionary will talk to you about the 51 Percent Solution.

The 51 Percent Solution says that if you do something more often than not, change will follow. You will have some days when you feel 100 percent on board and others when you want to snuggle into the past. As long as, 51 percent of the time, you take the new step, you will get to your destination. The conservative tendency of the brain then becomes your ally because each time you practice the new habit, you strengthen the neural pathways that support it. Over time, 51 percent becomes 60, 70, 80 percent…and you have created a new normal.

Predicting the Pitfalls

What are some of the thinking and feeling habits that inhibit change? We'd like to explore with you a number of "failure paths" we have identified. Engaging in these mental, emotional, and social behaviors more than 50 percent of the time will lead your change path to a dead end. Do you recognize any of them? We offer some alternative thoughts, feelings, and actions, in case one of your failure paths has turned into such a deep rut that you can't see any other choices.

Failure Paths	Failure Thoughts	Success Factors
Perfectionistic, *all or nothing* thinking	*Unless I do all of it consistently every day, there's no point in doing anything.*	Consider many options. Remember the 51 Percent Solution.
Lack of hope or discouragement related to self-doubt	*I've tried so many times; why should this be any different? Other people have what it takes, but I don't.*	Remember past successes. Open to new possibilities.

Lack of external support and listening to "saboteurs"	*It's weak to need other people; I should be able to do this on my own.* *My mother thinks I should just snap out it.*	Engage a team. Honestly assess other people's investment in your staying the same and limit contact with those who don't support your changing.
Fear of the unknown: *What will I be like without depression?*	*People will expect so much more of me if I'm not depressed.*	Tolerate distress/discomfort: learn to recognize the voice of fear and breathe into the places in your body where you feel the discomfort.
Getting stuck in thinking	*I'm not sure I'm really ready to do this yet. Once I understand why I'm depressed, I'll be able to be different.*	Move from thinking into doing. Take the smallest next step in a direction aligned with your intention.
Blaming externals	*I can't meditate, my kids/cat/dog/telephone won't leave me alone.*	Take ownership of your own choices. Ask for help. Develop a realistic plan that honors the limitations of your current situation. Get creative. For example, if you have small children, let diaper changing be an opportunity to practice mindfulness.
Novelty wearing off	*I've lost my enthusiasm. This is hard, and it's getting boring, and I keep forgetting to take my supplements.*	Reevaluate your approach. Try something new. Change your schedule. Invite another to join you or give you new ideas. Recognize and reward yourself for small steps.

The critic will try to shame you for every place you see yourself in the above failure paths. Listen instead to the visionary, who says, "Although it looks like there is a dividing line between the failure paths and the success factors, that line is actually a bridge."

Connecting with your visionary, fill out the following table. Use the failure paths in the table above or add your own.

Failure Paths	Failure Thoughts	Success Factors

Supporting Your Changing Self

How can you nourish your best intentions while also being mindful of the power of resistance? An old Cherokee story can illuminate this question.

An elderly Cherokee elder was teaching his grandchildren about life. He said to them, "A fight is going on inside me. It is a terrible fight, and it is between two wolves. One wolf is evil: he is fear, anger, envy, sorrow, regret, greed, arrogance, self-pity, guilt, resentment, inferiority, lies, false pride, competition, superiority, and ego. The other is good: he is joy, peace, love, hope, sharing, serenity, humility, kindness, benevolence, friendship, empathy, generosity, truth, compassion, and faith. This same fight is going on inside you and inside every other person, too." They thought about it for a minute, and then one child asked his grandfather, "Which wolf will win, Grandfather?" The elder simply replied, "The one you feed the most."

We could say that one wolf is our fear, our doubt, our resistance, our despair, our moments of passivity or helplessness or depressed mood. The other wolf carries our positive intention, our longing for change, our knowledge of our own abilities to create that change, and the willingness to make efforts, however small, to make change happen.

The following list suggests a few ways that you could feed the part of yourself that wants to change and is capable of making change happen:

Recall your intention. Yogi Berra is said to have noted, "If you don't know where you're going, you'll end up somewhere else!" Clearly stating your intention as you have done in the vision board exercise will steer you in the right direction. Your intention can be a "work in progress," and regularly revisited.

Remember what you're already doing well. In chapter 1 you completed the resilience skills questionnaire. Anytime resistance or discouragement shows up, it pays to remember what's gone well and the skills you have but may have forgotten about.

Cultivate willingness. Resistance is all about closing down; willingness is the essence of staying open. At times you may need to simply "be willing to be willing" to entertain new information or take a new action or ask for what you need. Any small opening will begin the process of moving past resistance.

Practice acceptance. An eleventh-century Tibetan story illustrates the power of acceptance:

One day Milarepa arrived home to find his cave filled with demons. They were wild and crazy demons, and disturbed his peace of mind. To get them to leave, he first tried telling them to get out using logic. No success. After multiple attempts to reason with them, he lost his temper, and ranted and raved. Still they stayed. Realizing his efforts to reason with them were doomed, he finally gave up and simply sat down. "Well, I'm not leaving and neither are you, it seems. I guess we'll just have to learn to get along," he said to them. Immediately all but the most vicious and threatening demon left. In a flash of wisdom, Milarepa approached the vicious demon and put his head directly into its mouth. "Eat me, then," he said. "I'm powerless to defeat you." With this, the demon left him in peace.

The moral of the story? When we simply and radically accept what's happening, the demon of resistance leaves us.

Sustain hope and faith. At times faith and hope are in short supply. Especially in the "lean times" or "thin places" that come with depression, it helps to tap into sources outside of yourself. Your spiritual tradition and practices, your supportive friends, inspiring stories and readings, and uplifting music can all be your allies.

Ask for support. The road to a more joyful life can be long, rocky, exhilarating, and beautiful. Sharing the trip with others can lighten the difficulties and enhance the joys. Finding a network of support—your travel companions—is essential.

BUILD YOUR CIRCLE OF SUPPORT

Take a few quiet moments to reflect on your current circle of support. Consider these questions:

- Who knows you best? Who is most completely accepting of you just as you are, and affirms your essential goodness? Place these people's names at the center of the concentric circles diagram on the following page.

- Whom do you know who has traveled this way before—who understands the struggle with depression but has made positive changes? Place these people's names in the next circle of the diagram.

- What professionals or organizations do you know of that you might consult with: therapists, clergy, support groups, educational programs? Place these names in the outside circle of the diagram.

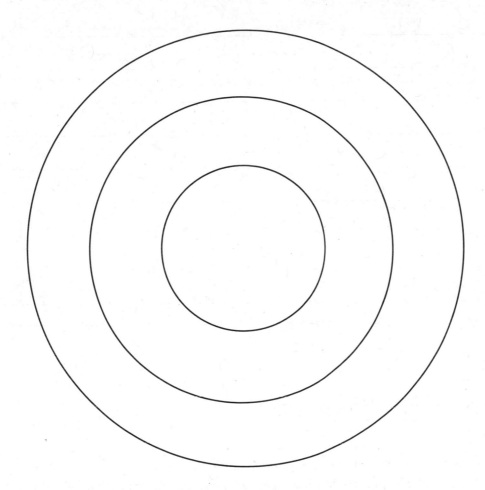

- Look over your diagram and see where you already have strong support and where it needs to be shored up. Create an action plan below for engaging these people or organizations as allies on the journey you are about to embark upon. Be specific: list their names and contact information, and include when and how you plan to contact them to enlist their help (direct conversation, phone call, e-mail, letter).

Name and Contact Information:

_____

_____

_____

_____

_____

Plan for Enlisting Support:

_____

_____

_____

_____

_____

_____   _____

_____   _____

_____   _____

_____   _____

_____   _____

_____   _____

_____   _____

_____   _____

_____   _____

SUMMING UP CHAPTER 2

- Change is a whole-person process—body, mind, and heart—and is most successful when grounded in self-acceptance. Self-improvement projects, often initiated by the inner critic, seldom lead to sustainable change.

- Effective change comes from aligning with your inner visionary: the part of yourself that sees your goodness and your potential, and works with you to make positive change.

- Because your human brain is wired for conservation and survival, changing habits and patterns can be challenging; you will encounter resistance to change. Rather than give up in the face of resistance, you can work with this natural component of the change process.

- It's not necessary to be perfect in your efforts to change. When trying something a new way, it's good enough to go the new way 51 percent of the time. Gradually you will find yourself moving toward the new and extinguishing the old. Change builds upon change. Small, persistent, new choices lead to transformation.

Part 2

The Body Pathways

Chapter 3

Nurturing:

Care for Your Body

Tell me what you eat and I will tell you who you are.

Anthelme Brillat-Savarin, 1826

"I had no idea that what I ate could make such a difference in how I feel! Now I see how it all fits together." Like most people, Jim thought he could think his way out of depression. He had done all the things he thought were important: cognitive therapy, nutritional supplements, and even medication. Yet he was still depressed until he realized how his eating habits were sabotaging his mood.

Like Jim, it is common to see depression as occurring solely in the mind. The mind has a strong influence, of course. But there are many other factors at work in creating inner emotional states, whether those are states of well-being or of distress. A depressed mood, for instance, becomes translated into experience through chemical messengers such as serotonin and dopamine: chemicals that are produced from the nutrients in food.

Healthy nutrients in food provide the information that the body needs to function as it was designed. Bad information, however, triggers destructive cascades that affect the whole body, eroding both physical and emotional resilience. As Jim discovered, what we eat has a profound impact on how we feel, either for better or for worse.

Because you need a solid physical foundation for brain resilience, the first gateway is to care for the body by feeding it properly. If additional support is needed, then nutritional supplements can be added, as we will describe in the next chapter. When even more potent support is required, as with severe symptoms of depression, then medications may be needed. Whatever else we do, we must remember that a well-nourished body provides the physical foundation for a joyful state of mind.

There are five common dietary roadblocks that may be fueling depression or preventing recovery:

- Poor-quality diet

- Blood sugar and insulin imbalance

- Faulty digestion

- Excess inflammation

- Food sensitivities and intolerances

The following pages will guide you through these potential barriers to resilience. You'll find a description of each roadblock, its impact on mood, and an assessment to help you determine if this is happening for you. If it is, don't worry—the brain is incredibly resilient, and we will give you proven strategies to remove these roadblocks to healing.

ROADBLOCK ONE: POOR-QUALITY DIET

Even in the healthiest of American diets, there is room for improvement. That's because the standard american diet (SAD) is sadly lacking in nutrients. Here are just a few examples:

- Many Americans have heeded the call to eat a low-fat diet, not realizing that the brain needs plenty of healthy fats to function well. Often those fat calories are replaced with sugar or refined carbohydrates that have a further negative impact on mood.

- Others eat excess amounts of fat, but still don't get enough of the brain-healthy omega-3 fats. That can be hard to do today, because the grains and animal products widely available have far fewer omega-3 fats than the foods eaten by our ancestors.

- Farming practices have eroded the soil in many areas, leaching out important micronutrients. You may think you are eating healthy foods, yet they can be missing key ingredients for neurotransmitter production.

- Many foods contain chemicals (including fertilizers, pesticides, hormones, and artificial colorings or flavorings) that send harmful information to the body, disrupting normal cell communication and function.

- Nature has designed an elegant package of nutrition in the form of whole foods. Refining and processing these foods removes many of the core nutrients that the brain needs. When whole wheat is processed, for instance, it loses about 75 percent of its vitamins and minerals and 95 percent of its fiber and fatty acids!

Ironically, in a country where most of us have plenty to eat, for many of us, our brains are starving for the nutrients they need. To find out what kind of information your diet is providing for a healthy brain, take this brief assessment.

Exercise: Assessing Your Diet

Circle the most appropriate answer. When you have finished with section A, continue on with section B. Then add up your numbers to get a sense of how your diet rates.

0—Never

1—Infrequently (almost never)

2—Occasionally (some of the time)

3—Frequently (most of the time)

4—Always

Section A

I eat 2–3 fruits daily.	0	1	2	3	4
I eat 2–3 vegetables daily.	0	1	2	3	4
I use olive oil, canola oil, or coconut oil.	0	1	2	3	4
I eat nuts and seeds daily.	0	1	2	3	4
I choose grass-fed beef or bison.	0	1	2	3	4

When eating beef, I choose 85 percent or more lean.	0	1	2	3	4
I drink at least six 8-ounce glasses of water daily.	0	1	2	3	4
When eating poultry, I choose natural poultry.	0	1	2	3	4
When consuming dairy, I choose hormone-free dairy.	0	1	2	3	4
I eat breakfast daily.	0	1	2	3	4

Select the Most Appropriate Number

Number of servings of green, leafy vegetables eaten each week	0	1	2	3	4+
Number of servings of legumes eaten each week	0	1	2	3	4+
Number of whole grains eaten per day	0	1	2	3	4+
Number of fish or seafood servings per week	0	1	2	3	4+
Number of calcium-rich foods eaten daily	0	1	2	3	4+

Add up total for section A.

Total _____

Section B

I drink three or more cups of caffeinated coffee daily.	0	1	2	3	4
I use artificial sweeteners.	0	1	2	3	4
I eat sugar-sweetened cereal daily.	0	1	2	3	4
I eat doughnuts, muffins, or pastry daily.	0	1	2	3	4
I eat candy in any form daily.	0	1	2	3	4
I eat at fast-food restaurants.	0	1	2	3	4
I eat cookies, cakes, or bars daily.	0	1	2	3	4

Select Most Appropriate Number

	0	1	2	3	4+
Number of servings of juice daily	0	1	2	3	4+
Number of soda/pop servings daily	0	1	2	3	4+
Number of diet soda/pop servings daily	0	1	2	3	4+
Number of glasses of beer (12 ounces) or wine (6 ounces) weekly	0	1	2	3	4+
Number of drinks (vodka, gin, whiskey, or other spirits) weekly	0	1	2	3	4+
Number of refined grains eaten daily	0	1	2	3	4+
Number of servings of chips eaten weekly	0	1	2	3	4+
Number of servings of bacon, ham, sausage eaten weekly	0	1	2	3	4+

Add numbers from section B.

Total _____

Section A identifies the positive information that food provides to your body. The higher the total in section A, the better your body works.

Section B highlights the parts of your diet that may have a negative influence, getting in the way of proper brain function. The higher your total in section B, the more strain you are placing on your body—and your mood.

Strategies for Improving Your Diet

It may seem obvious that increasing your number in section A and reducing your number in section B will be good for your health—and your mood. Most of us know what foods are healthful. But there is a gap between knowing and doing, partly because there is so much confusing and conflicting information about diet.

Eating well is simpler than it seems. If you have good digestion and eat natural, unprocessed foods, you will get the information you need to nourish your body and brain. The following lists will help simplify your food choices.

FOODS TO INCLUDE

- Fresh plant foods, including fruits and vegetables (5 to 13 daily)

- Whole-grain, high-fiber foods such as brown rice, wild rice, buckwheat, barley, quinoa, whole wheat, and oats

- Chicken, lean cuts of grass-fed red meat when available

- Fatty fish—especially salmon, sardines, trout, and tuna

- Dairy products—butter and cheeses in moderation

- Olive oil, flaxseeds, and avocados

- Legumes—especially soybeans, lentils, white beans, black beans, chickpeas

- Nuts such as walnuts, almonds, pecans, and Brazil nuts

- Fresh and dried herbs

FOODS TO REDUCE OR AVOID

- Foods high in refined sugar, such as candy, soda pop, pastries

- Processed foods and refined products like white bread, instant potatoes, and chips

- Trans-fatty acids such as partially hydrogenated oils

- Omega-6 fatty-acid oils such as corn, sunflower, and soybean oils

- Saturated fat in animal fats

- Corn syrup and high-fructose corn syrup

- Foods containing artificial sweeteners and artificial colorings or flavorings

- Artificial preservatives such as MSG and BHT

ROADBLOCK TWO: BLOOD SUGAR–INSULIN IMBALANCE

Carbohydrates are foods that get broken down into glucose molecules, also known as blood sugar. A "simple carbohydrate" gets released as glucose very quickly, whereas a "complex carbohydrate" is released more slowly. In this case, slow is good; it is much easier for the body to process a steady supply of blood sugar.

Each cell in the body has its own energy plant, and glucose is the fuel used for energy production. But the cells somehow have to get glucose out of the bloodstream and inside their cell membranes. That is the job of the pancreas and its hormone, insulin.

Insulin travels to the outside of the cells and "parks" on the insulin receptor sites. Once there, insulin acts like a delivery truck that carries glucose into the cells. Because this process is so important, the body works very hard to maintain the balance between glucose and insulin.

This balance is disrupted if glucose enters the bloodstream too quickly—after a "sugar binge," for instance. In response to this flood of sugar, the pancreas sends out an excessive amount of insulin, which quickly takes glucose out of the bloodstream and into the cells. Now you have two problems: blood sugar has rapidly dropped, and there are a lot of insulin delivery trucks circulating with nothing to do. The crucial glucose-insulin balance has been upset, causing the brain to send out distress signals that say, "Get more sugar—now!" This does what any internal emergency would do: it sets off the alarms and raises the level of the stress hormones.

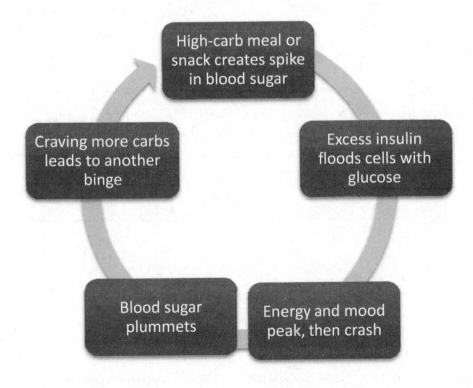

Insulin Resistance

If this imbalanced pattern of excess glucose–excess insulin continues, the insulin receptor sites eventually begin to shut down and glucose cannot be delivered into the cells. This is a longer-term problem known as *insulin resistance*.

Insulin resistance has a much bigger impact on mood than most people realize. When it is present, the brain cannot efficiently make dopamine, one of the feel-good brain chemicals. And since it is so hard to get glucose inside the cells, they cannot make enough energy, leaving you feeling sluggish and lethargic.

With insulin resistance, it is as if the cells are starving in a sea of plenty. You can eat a lot of food, there may be plenty of sugar in the bloodstream, yet you can still develop symptoms of low blood sugar, including:

- Dizziness

- Headache

- Excessive sweating

- Fatigue

- Restlessness

- Difficulty concentrating

- Frustration, anger, and irritability

Eating a meal of highly processed, calorie-dense, nutrient-depleted foods can cause exaggerated spikes in blood sugar and lipids. This state, called *postprandial dysmetabolism*, creates immediate oxidative stress (excess free radicals). This increase in free radicals acutely triggers inflammation, decreases serotonin, and disrupts sleep and energy—all of which impact mood (O'Keefe, Geewala, and O'Keefe 2008).

• *Debra's Story*

"I feel like Dr. Jekyll and Mr. Hyde," announced Debra as she plopped down in the chair. She couldn't concentrate, felt anxious, and had a "short fuse," but her biggest concerns were her mood swings, along with increased appetite and low energy—and her uncontrollable sugar cravings.

We looked at her diet and found that she usually skipped breakfast because she could not get out of bed early enough. Lunch tended to be organic pasta with red sauce and an apple. Debra noted that she was usually extremely hungry by late afternoon and early evening, when she arrived home from work. She frequently had crackers and a glass of wine while making dinner at around 7:00 p.m. "Usually I do so well during the day, and then I really crave foods, especially carbs, in the evening."

She began her recovery by including a protein-rich breakfast. She was sugar sensitive, so she needed to eat smaller, more frequent meals throughout the day. We suggested that she add protein to lunch, and identified a late-afternoon "mini-meal" that would blunt the effect of the energy slump and evening cravings for sugar.

Four weeks later, when Debra returned for a follow-up, she reported doing very well and proclaimed: "My mood swings have all but disappeared—and I've lost five pounds!" She was able to reduce the caffeine and sugar she depended upon for energy. "I couldn't believe how well it worked. I feel so balanced and light."

Assessing Your Glucose-Insulin Balance

Place a check mark next to all of the items that apply to you:

☐ I get headaches that are helped by eating.

☐ I feel impatient or angry between meals.

☐ I crave sweets.

☐ Once I eat sweets, I can't seem to stop.

☐ I crash in the afternoon.

☐ I eat something sweet in the afternoon.

☐ I skip breakfast regularly.

☐ I sometimes skip lunch.

☐ I eat bagels, cereal, or pastries for breakfast.

☐ I have difficulty concentrating.

☐ I have panic attacks.

☐ I have a family history of diabetes.

☐ I have a family history of alcohol dependence.

☐ I have a family history of obesity.

☐ I feel shaky or faint when I don't eat frequently.*

☐ I feel tired most of the time.

☐ I feel sleepy after I eat a carbohydrate-rich meal.

☐   I am especially hungry in the evening.

☐   I can't seem to lose weight no matter what I do.

☐   I have a diagnosis of ADD or ADHD.*

☐   I have diabetes.*

☐   I am alcohol dependent.*

☐   I am obese.*

If you checked fewer than three boxes, follow the general recommendations listed below. If you checked three or more boxes or if you placed a check mark next to *any* of the issues with an asterisk, include the supplements listed to improve insulin and glucose balance.

Strategies for Improving Glucose-Insulin Balance

Balancing blood sugar and correcting insulin resistance are among the most effective dietary strategies for influencing mood. It is possible to regain the correct balance of insulin and glucose, and thereby lift your mood and energy by what you eat.

GENERAL RECOMMENDATIONS

- Eat every three to four hours, for example, 7:30 a.m., 11:30 a.m., 3:30 p.m., 6:30 p.m.

- Never skip a meal or a snack, even if you are not that hungry. Nibble on something small just to assure a steady flow of energy and avoid a blood sugar crash.

- Favor complex carbohydrates that are also high-fiber foods; they take longer to be broken down into simple sugars.

- Never eat grain by itself; always eat grains with protein and fat. For instance, if you are having a piece of toast, have an egg or put almond butter on the toast.

FOODS TO INCLUDE

- High-fiber, complex carbohydrates; fruits, vegetables, legumes, and whole grains promote slower delivery of glucose.

- Quality protein and fats with each meal; they slow the delivery of glucose and help avoid spikes in insulin.

- Monounsaturated fats, such as olive oil, slow things down as well.

- One-fourth to half a teaspoon of cinnamon daily helps increase insulin sensitivity (Qin, Panickar, and Anderson 2010).

FOODS TO REDUCE OR AVOID

- Simple carbohydrates and highly refined and processed foods such as white breads and pastries, white pastas, white potatoes, and candy.

- Alcohol, which is a concentrated sugar.

- Diet soda; artificial sweeteners cause an unhealthy insulin response (Nettleton et al. 2009).

- Avoid high-fructose corn syrup; it causes sugar cravings because it fails to give you a signal (via a chemical messenger called leptin) that you are full (Bray, Nielson, and Popkin 2004).

SUPPLEMENTS FOR INSULIN-GLUCOSE BALANCE

- Magnesium: 500 mg daily

- Fish oil: 1,000 mg daily

- Alpha lipoic acid: 500 mg daily (improves insulin sensitivity)

- Chromium picolinate: 200 mcg twice daily (helps curb cravings)

ROADBLOCK THREE: FAULTY DIGESTION

The job of the digestive system is to break food down into smaller substances that can then be absorbed into the body. Vitamins, minerals, and other compounds are "liberated" during digestion, making them available to do their jobs. Unfortunately, many people are at risk for nutrient deficiencies—even if they eat the right foods—because their poor digestion doesn't allow the release and absorption of key nutrients.

Poor digestion has several impacts on health and mood:

Impaired immunity: The immune system—70 percent of which resides in the gut—functions poorly when digestion is faulty. Also, stomach acid is necessary to destroy microbes.

Nutrient deficiencies: When stomach acid is low (for example, from acid-reducing medications or chronic stress), it can affect the breakdown of protein and B vitamins needed to make neurotransmitters.

Inflammation: Faulty digestion creates messengers of inflammation, resulting in bodily pain and ineffective brain-chemical production.

> The intestinal lining has a layer of cells that acts as a barrier, preventing bacteria from entering the bloodstream through the intestine. But if these cells weaken from exposure to toxins or from poor diet, the barrier becomes permeable, allowing bacteria to leak through the intestinal wall and create an inflammatory response. This may cause symptoms such as fatigue or a general sense of being unwell. It has also been linked to major depression. A 2008 study found that the prevalence of "leaky gut" was significantly higher in those with major depression than in healthy volunteers. It is recommended that patients with major depression be checked and, if necessary, treated for intestinal permeability (Maes, Kubera, and Leunis 2008).

• Todd's Story

Todd's mood was deteriorating rapidly, and he felt increasingly anxious. His digestion was interfering with all aspects of his life: "I am so busy; I don't have time for this digestive stuff. I can't even exercise." He had lost his appetite because when he ate, he developed painful acid reflux or heartburn.

Todd had been diagnosed with GERD (gastrointestinal reflux disease) two years before and started taking Prilosec (omeprazole), an acid-reducing medication, which was gradually being increased due to his lack of response.

He said he'd always had gas, bloating, and "sluggish" bowels, sometimes going three days without a bowel movement. We suspected too little stomach acid rather than too much, and we began supplements to improve digestion: a probiotic, digestive enzymes, and a trial of warm lemon water. Todd began to feel better, and then he conducted a modified elimination diet. He discovered that he reacted to nightshades (white potatoes, tomatoes, peppers, and eggplant) with bloating, cramping, and gas.

Todd avoided the nightshade vegetables for a time and gradually tapered off his acid-reducing medication under his doctor's supervision. We also addressed Todd's stress, which was contributing to his digestive issues and anxiety. He felt as if he were on high alert all the time, so turning down his stress response (as you will learn to do later in this workbook) was vital in his turnaround.

When seen for a follow-up visit, Todd reported, "I feel calm again; I'm practically back to normal. I'm back at the gym, and I've even found time to coach my son's baseball team."

Assessing Your Digestion

Place a check mark next to all of the items that apply to you:

- ☐ I take medication for acid reflux.

- ☐ I use over-the-counter antacids frequently.

- ☐ I have heartburn.

- ☐ I have nausea.

- ☐ I have a sour stomach.

- ☐ I have chronic diarrhea or loose stools.

- ☐ I experience constipation or a sluggish bowel.

- ☐ I frequently feel bloated.

- ☐ I burp or pass gas frequently.

- ☐ I have stomach pain.

- ☐ I am aware of my breath odor.

- ☐ I have chronic yeast infections.

- ☐ I feel nauseous when I take a multivitamin.

- ☐ I have used antibiotics more than once in the past year.

- ☐ I have a history of frequent antibiotic use.

- ☐ I use aspirin, ibuprofen, or other NSAIDs.

- ☐ I have canker sores.

- ☐ I have irritable bowel syndrome.*

- ☐ I have celiac disease.*

- ☐ I have Crohn's disease.*

If you checked fewer than three boxes, simply follow the strategies listed next. If you checked three or more boxes or if you placed a check mark next to *any* of the issues with an asterisk, it is recommended that you also conduct the elimination challenge (see roadblock five) to determine if a food sensitivity is having an influence on your digestion and mood.

Strategies for Improving Digestion

If you choose to eat healthy foods, then it is up to the crucial process of digestion to determine which nutrients reach the bloodstream and eventually give the brain the ingredients it needs to remain healthy and balanced. The following suggestions will help assure that you are actually liberating the nutrients that you are consuming.

- Be sure you are drinking enough water. Dehydration brings the digestive tract to a screeching halt.

- Chew, chew, and chew some more. Saliva breaks down carbohydrates, and there are hormones released when chewing that increase the activity of the immune system.

- If you are taking acid-reducing medication, talk with your provider to determine a possible schedule to taper off the medication while identifying the underlying cause of the heartburn or reflux.

- Drink apple cider vinegar (1 to 2 teaspoons in 8 ounces of water) or warm lemon water with meals to aid in digestion and help with the movement of the gastrointestinal tract.

- Consider possible causes of inflammation, such as food sensitivities. Conduct an elimination challenge to determine if this is an issue (discussed in detail later in the chapter).

- Add a probiotic supplement to help rebalance the good bacteria, which will help normalize your elimination. Be sure the supplement has multiple strains of bacteria such as acidophilus, bifidobacteria, lactobacillus, and fructooligosaccharide (FOS, a natural sweetener that supports healthy gut bacteria).

- Take a fiber supplement containing psyllium.

- Add ground flaxseed and chia seeds.

- Drink teas made from ginger, peppermint, cinnamon, and licorice root.

- Focus on the following digestion-supporting foods:

  - Grains such as buckwheat, steel-cut oats, barley, wild rice

- Fresh vegetables, particularly kale, carrots, cabbage, cauliflower, squash, and broccoli

- Fresh fruit, particularly pears, apples, plums, bananas, berries, and cherries

- Cultured foods such as yogurt, kefir, and milk

ROADBLOCK FOUR: EXCESS INFLAMMATION

Inflammation is important; it helps to defend the body against challenges such as injury, trauma, infection, allergens, and toxins. Too much inflammation, however, is harmful. Excess inflammation in the joints, for example, can cause arthritis; inflammation in the airways leads to an asthma attack. When the inflammation occurs in the brain, it can affect neurotransmitters such as serotonin and dopamine, aggravating depression.

Current research suggests that stressful life events can bring about symptoms of a depressed mood by physically damaging the brain. This damage triggers a repair response (not unlike any wound repair) that includes inflammation. The changes caused by these inflammatory messengers may lead to physical pain and a "depression" of normal function during the repair process. When these repair processes continue for longer periods, due to ongoing stress or an inability to fully repair, depressive symptoms can become chronic. In the body, everything truly is connected (Smith 2011).

Evidence linking alterations in brain chemistry to inflammation is building. People with depression are shown to have increased levels of inflammatory cytokines (the chemical messengers of inflammation), which have been linked to changes in sleep, fatigue, irritability, sadness, and impaired concentration. Elevated cytokines may even make it less likely that you will respond to antidepressant treatment (Miller, Maletic, and Raison 2010).

- *Lynn's Story*

"When my daughter asked if I was mad at her, I knew things had to change." Lynn's first depression occurred after she stopped drinking sixteen years ago. Now she felt it returning. After a difficult eight-year marriage, Lynn was now a divorced, single parent of a seven-year-old daughter. She worked full-time. She was sleeping too much but still felt very fatigued. Even though she had been recovered for sixteen years and no longer craved alcohol, Lynn found herself craving other sugars.

Lynn also had a long history of inflammation. She had had eczema as a child and severe acne as a teenager. Her skin was extremely dry. Recently she was experiencing more frequent headaches.

As a first step, we conducted an elimination challenge to determine if Lynn had underlying food sensitivities. When she returned after doing the challenge, she said she felt "so much better." She had more energy, no headaches, and clearer skin. She was less irritable, saying, "Even my seven-year-old daughter noticed." She had a strong reaction to dairy products from cows, both milk and cheeses. They caused her to feel as if she were in a fog, made her feel crabby, and gave her a persistent two-day headache. Dairy also intensified her cravings for sugar.

Because of her dry skin and mood issues, we also started her on a fish-oil (omega-3 fatty acid) supplement and other anti-inflammatory foods.

Lynn returned twelve weeks later and said she continued to be symptom free. "It was hard at first but well worth it."

Assessing Inflammation

Place a check mark next to all of the symptoms that apply to you:

☐ Headaches

☐ Acne

☐ Hives or rashes

☐ Dry or flaky skin

☐ Asthma

☐ Chest congestion

☐ Joint pain

☐ Muscle pain

☐ Frequent infections

☐ Bags or dark circles under eyes

☐ Stuffy nose

☐ Sinus congestion

☐ Excess mucus

☐ Frequent need to clear throat

☐ Chronic cough

☐ Hoarseness

☐ Sore throat

☐ Swollen gums

☐ Arthritis

☐ Canker sores

☐ Eczema or psoriasis*

☐ Frequent sinus infections*

☐ Irritable bowel syndrome*

☐ Colitis or Crohn's disease*

☐ Hypothyroidism*

☐ Autoimmune disease such as rheumatoid arthritis, lupus, or Raynaud's disease.*

If you checked fewer than three boxes, follow the general recommendations listed below. If you checked three or more boxes or if you placed a check mark next to *any* of the issues with an asterisk, it is recommended that you also conduct the elimination challenge (roadblock five) to determine if a food sensitivity is causing inflammation or influencing your mood.

Strategies for Offsetting Inflammation

Because of the destructive impact of inflammation on the brain, reducing it is a primary strategy for improving your mood. The following recommendations include general strategies for reducing inflammation that can be helpful for everyone. When you address roadblocks two and five (glucose-insulin balance and food sensitivities), you are also cooling down inflammation.

GENERAL RECOMMENDATIONS

- Pay attention to the types of fat in your diet. Omega-6 fats (including most cooking oils, such as corn, sunflower, safflower, and soybean) promote inflammation, while omega-3 fats reduce it. We need both, and our ancestors had about a one-to-one ratio between them. Now we eat so many more omega-6 fats that the ratio is closer to twenty to one. So while we can turn inflammation on, we have trouble turning it off again.

- Reduce intake of omega-6 fats by limiting corn, safflower, sunflower, and soybean oils. Instead, use:

  - olive oil for most cooking

  - grapeseed oil for high-heat cooking

  - olive and flax oils for salad dressings

- Omega-3 fatty acids (EPA and DHA) decrease the production of pro-inflammatory messengers (cytokines). They also help build healthy brain membranes and allow normal communication between cells.

- Increase intake of omega-3 fatty acids by eating:

  - cold-water fish: salmon, halibut, mackerel, herring, tuna, and sardines; cod-liver oil or other fish-oil supplements

  - nuts and seeds: walnuts, pumpkin seeds, and freshly ground flaxseeds or flax oil

  - wild game, seaweed, algae, and eggs from flax-fed chickens

- Vitamin C: found in citrus fruits, tomatoes, green leafy vegetables, parsley, cabbage, asparagus, avocados, cantaloupe, currants, mangoes, kiwi, papaya, peppers, cherries, pineapple, and strawberries.

- Curcumin is a naturally occurring yellow pigment found in the spice turmeric that has been used for thousands of years in indigenous medicine for the management of inflammatory disorders and wound healing. You can add it to soups, stir-fries, and rice dishes.

- Eat plenty of onions, garlic, and ginger—all known for their anti-inflammatory activity.

- Soy products such as tofu, miso, edamame, and tempeh may also reduce inflammation.

FOODS TO REDUCE

- Certain fats can cause inflammation in the body. Limit your intake of meats, poultry, whole milk, cream, butter, and cheese. Corn-fed animals have more pro-inflammatory fatty acids than grass-fed or free-range animals.

- Trans-fatty acids and partially hydrogenated vegetable oil also carry a pro-inflammatory message to your body's cells. Food labels now have to include the amount of trans fat per serving and list partially hydrogenated vegetable oil among the ingredients. Minimize your use of:

  - margarine

  - processed baked goods, crackers, and deep-fried foods

- Simple sugars and refined carbohydrates can create an inflammatory environment in the body. Do your best to limit your intake of them.

ROADBLOCK FIVE: FOOD SENSITIVITIES

There are often hidden saboteurs in our diets that make us feel miserable. It may even be a food that we eat frequently, but if we are sensitive to a particular food, the body will deal with it as an "invader": it will activate the immune system and create inflammation throughout the body. Ironically, you may even crave the very food to which you are sensitive, because the offending food can give you a momentary high. Food cravings, in fact, may provide useful clues about food sensitivities.

These are not true allergies, like those that some people have to nuts or shellfish. Food sensitivities are subtler than allergies, which makes them harder to discover. Sensitivity to foods can trigger joint pain, headaches, psoriasis, sinus congestion, and digestive disorders—*and* depression.

If you checked multiple issues when you assessed your digestion (roadblock three) or inflammation (roadblock four), you may want to conduct an elimination challenge to determine the potential culprit. The most common food intolerances are dairy, wheat, nightshade vegetables, and corn. If you suspect any food sensitivity based upon your assessment, follow the elimination-challenge diet below. You may discover a hidden food sensitivity that could unlock your normal digestion and dramatically reduce inflammation and depression. It is challenging but may be well worth the effort; you might even conclude that it's kind of fun!

The Elimination-Challenge Diet

For the initial ten days, you eliminate the foods listed below. Beginning on day eleven, you will begin to "challenge" one new food at a time.

FOODS TO ELIMINATE

- Dairy: We use two different categories for dairy—those containing mostly whey protein (milk, cream, sour cream, butter, and ice cream) and those containing mostly casein (cheese and yogurt).

- Wheat: Most bread and pasta, most flour, baked goods, durum, semolina, and farina. It is important to note that this does not mean gluten free. Gluten intolerance is an altogether different sensitivity. There is gluten in wheat, but there is also gluten in rye, spelt, and barley, which are allowed. You will simply be avoiding wheat. In fact you do not want to consume packaged gluten-free items, as they tend to contain corn flour and potato flour.

- Nightshade vegetables: White potatoes (meaning white-fleshed potatoes, including Yukon Gold and red potatoes), tomatoes, peppers, eggplant.

- Corn: Corn chips, corn tortillas, popcorn, corn oil, and corn syrup and other corn sweeteners; Splenda, sucralose, sorbitol, and xanthan gum are all made from corn.

You should also eliminate "white foods" (white breads, pasta, cookies, and cake), and avoid grain alcohol and beer. Many are made with wheat and corn.

You may encounter some unpleasant withdrawal symptoms, such as irritability, headaches, fatigue, or any of your usual mood symptoms. They will resolve within the first few days. Eat every three to four hours to avoid food cravings.

Keep a journal of how you feel from day one through to the end of the challenges. Note symptoms, lack of symptoms, sleep, and energy.

A key to the challenge is to focus on foods you *can* have. You are free to include any of the following foods during the challenge:

- Cereals: Oatmeal, oat bran, granola, cream of rye, puffed rice, puffed millet, or crispy brown rice with almond milk, soy milk, hemp milk, or rice milk.

- Cheese: Goat cheeses and goat milk, goat butter, and goat yogurt; sheep cheese.

- Coconut milk, coconut kefir, and coconut creamer.

- Grains: Rye, oat, or spelt bread made without wheat; rice cakes, rice crackers, and rye crackers; buckwheat or soba noodles, spelt pasta, brown rice pasta, brown rice, white rice, wild rice, oats, barley, millet, buckwheat groats, amaranth, and quinoa.

- Legumes: All legumes, including black beans, white beans, lentils, chickpeas, navy beans, and fava beans.

- Vegetables: All vegetables are fine to eat except corn, peppers, white potatoes, tomatoes, and eggplant. Sweet potatoes and yams are fine.

- Fruit: All fruit is fine.

- Protein: All eggs, poultry, fish, and meat. Beef and pork or other protein you normally eat can be included.

- Nuts and seeds: All nuts and seeds and nut butters unless an allergy is known.

- Oils and fats: All oils and fats are to be included except butter, margarine, and corn oil. Use mainly olive oil, canola oil, sesame oil, safflower oil, coconut oil, or peanut oil.

CHALLENGING ELIMINATED FOODS

After ten days it is time to reintroduce eliminated foods by testing, or "challenging," one new food at a time. When you test a food, you should eat *relatively large amounts* of it (between five and six servings). People frequently wonder if eating so many servings of a food in a day will cause a reaction. And the answer is no—the amount of food does not matter. You may feel full of corn or wheat, for instance, but no reaction will occur unless you are sensitive to it.

Reactions can include common and familiar symptoms or symptoms you've never had before, such as retaining water, or having itchy skin or a rash. Even if you think there is another explanation for how you are feeling (for example, "I am so tired today because I didn't sleep well last night"), you should still take note. You may not have slept well because you challenged with corn the day before and your body reacted as if there were an enemy on board. Reactions can also include mood symptoms like depression, irritability, or anxiety.

Day 11:   *Dairy (whey)*: Milk, ice cream (without corn syrup), sour cream, and butter.

Day 12:   Wait-and-see day. Follow regular elimination: no corn, wheat, dairy, or nightshades. Note any type of reaction.

Day 13:   Wait-and-see day. Follow regular elimination: no corn, wheat, dairy, or nightshades. Note any type of reaction.

Day 14:   *Dairy (casein)*: Any kind of cheese, cottage cheese, and natural yogurt.

Day 15:   Wait-and-see day. Follow regular elimination: no corn, wheat, dairy, or nightshades. Note any type of reaction.

Day 16:   Wait-and-see day. Follow regular elimination: no corn, wheat, dairy, or nightshades. Note any type of reaction.

Day 17:   *Wheat*: Use whole-wheat cereal, whole-wheat crackers, whole-wheat pasta, and whole-wheat breadsticks.

Day 18:   Wait-and-see day. Follow regular elimination: no corn, wheat, dairy, or nightshades. Note any type of reaction.

Day 19:   Wait-and-see day. Follow regular elimination: no corn, wheat, dairy, or nightshades. Note any type of reaction.

Day 20:   *Nightshades*: Potatoes, tomatoes, peppers, and eggplant. (If tomatoes or peppers give you heartburn or indigestion, only use potatoes when challenging.)

Day 21:   Wait-and-see day. Follow regular elimination: no corn, wheat, dairy, or nightshades. Note any type of reaction.

Day 22:   Wait-and-see day. Follow regular elimination: no corn, wheat, dairy, or nightshades. Note any type of reaction.

Day 23:   *Corn*: Use fresh ears of corn, frozen corn, popcorn (natural), or corn chips.

Day 24:   Wait-and-see day. Follow regular elimination: no corn, wheat, dairy, or nightshades. Note any type of reaction.

Day 25:   Wait-and-see day. Follow regular elimination: no corn, wheat, dairy, or nightshades. Note any type of reaction.

If you reacted to a food, you should avoid it for an additional eight weeks. After the eight-week period, you can begin to rotate the food back into your diet slowly to find out how often you can eat it without having a reaction. Start by eating the food once a week, then once every six days, and then five days; and finally, settle on rotating that food into your diet once every four days. As you can see, having a food sensitivity is not a sentence to never having that food again, but it is a message to be mindful about it.

TRACKING YOUR PROGRESS

Research shows that simply *intending* to change doesn't work very well. Having a goal doesn't do it either. What research *has* shown is that when people make a concrete plan, track their progress, and see themselves as successful, they are far more likely to carry out their goal.

For example, a recent study aimed to increase the consumption of fruits among college students. All 177 participating students were asked to set the goal of consuming more fruits for a seven-day period. They were randomly assigned to four groups. One group simply had the goal. Another group had the goal and some idea of how they would implement the goal. A third group imagined themselves being successful. The fourth group was asked to set the goal, to make a concrete plan, write it down (when, where, and how they would buy, prepare, and eat the fruit), *and* visualize themselves being successful. This last group ate twice as much fruit as any of the others (Knauper et al. 2011).

We encourage you to make use of this insight when you make your own goals, remembering that action is a critical step in the process of change. We suggest setting a few simple but specific goals, developing a concrete plan, and then tracking your progress. Be sure to make your goals both clear and achievable, and limit the number of goals you are working on at any time. You are far more likely to reach all of your goals if you can focus on just one or two at once. After achieving one goal, move on to another. To give yourself an extra boost, remember to visualize yourself being successful.

Recording honestly (remember, acceptance of who and where you are right now!) will give you a great understanding of where you succeed and where you get stuck. At some point down the road, you can refer to this log for insight and ideas on how to move forward.

Remember, your goals should reflect where you are in the process and your skills so far. For instance, if you already eat balanced, frequent meals, your goal may be to add variety to your choices in vegetables. If, on the other hand, you are someone who "grazes" most of the day, your goal could be to eat breakfast daily and identify two to three food choices that could be rotated, so you don't eat the same thing every day.

The tracking tool below has space for you to list both your goals and the action steps you take toward achieving them, as well as your progress. Additional copies of this form can be downloaded from nhpubs.com/22256 and filled out for the chapters that follow, allowing you to add new goals for each pathway. (Note: If you wish, you can also photocopy the form, or develop a version of it that suits your needs.) *Being intentional and accountable in a written way can be highly motivating.*

After the tracking tool you will find an example of how it might be filled in for this chapter.

WHOLE-PERSON CHANGE-TRACKING TOOL

GOALS AND ACTIONS

Here is where you record your concrete plan. Set a clear goal and write it down along with two or three specific action steps. Then record your progress for each action step. Repeat this process with any other goals you set for this pathway.

Goal: _____

Action step: _____

Progress: _____

_____

_____

_____

Action step: _____

Progress: _____

_____

_____

_____

Action step: _____

Progress: _____

_____

_____

_____

REFLECTIONS

Record your insights, emotional responses, and thoughts about where you might go next. Include any ideas from the chapter that you would like to remember. Note any challenges you are experiencing as you move toward your goals, as well as potential solutions.

_____

_____

_____

_____

_____

_____

_____

_____

_____

_____

SAMPLE WHOLE-PERSON CHANGE-TRACKING TOOL

GOALS AND ACTIONS

Goal: _I will stabilize my blood sugar._

Action step: _Reduce diet soda, one every day._

Progress: _I had only two diet sodas today._

Action step: _Eat breakfast, either a smoothie or eggs._

Progress: _I had eggs and toast for breakfast today, and noticed that I was mentally clearer._

Action step: _Protein every time I eat._

Progress: _I included protein with all my meals today, but not with my afternoon snack._

REFLECTIONS

Will increase awareness and read labels of foods that are premade.

With type 2 diabetes in family history and sugar cravings, learned blood sugar and insulin imbalance could be sabotaging my mood.

Had higher scores in the inflammation assessment, so am thinking about doing the elimination-challenge after the holidays to determine if I have a food sensitivity.

Stay connected to my visionary, not my critic.

SUMMING UP CHAPTER 3

- A well-nourished body provides a foundation for a joyful state of mind.

- Food provides information that can have either positive or negative effects on the body. Healthy nutrients in food provide signals for the body to function in the way it was designed to.

- There are five dietary "roadblocks" that may be fueling anxiety, depression, or other stress-related mood issues:

  - poor overall diet

  - blood sugar imbalance

  - faulty digestion

  - excess inflammation

  - food sensitivities and intolerance

Chapter 4

Balancing:

Support Your Brain

*If depression is creeping up and must be faced, learn something about
the nature of the beast: you may escape without a mauling.*

Dr. W. R. Shepherd

"**M**y friends are telling me to try medications, but I don't know. I hear others complaining about side effects or not being sure that they are really helpful. I try to eat right and exercise. Isn't there something else I can do?"

When diet and lifestyle alone are not enough to sustain a healthy mood, we believe it is best to discover where the brain imbalance lies and then try to remedy that through the intelligent addition of nutritional supplements. If that still falls short, then medication, used wisely and judiciously, may provide symptom relief as you work toward more natural, sustainable, and healthy brain function.

This chapter will give you all the tools you need to create your own resilient-brain program, along with just enough brain science to help you understand how things work to sustain your mood, what can go wrong, and what you can do about it. After working through this chapter, you will be able to:

- Identify the three subtypes of depression, using questionnaires to help you determine whether you tend toward one of these types.

- Decide if you are likely to have a particular brain-chemical imbalance and understand its consequences.

- Create your own personalized supplement program to establish a solid nutritional foundation and help restore balance.

- Know when medications are needed and which are your best choices given your type of brain chemical imbalance.

This chapter contains a lot of information that can feel overwhelming. Remember that this is a process, and you don't have to change everything at once or do things perfectly. The chapter is organized around three distinctly different subtypes of depression, so you can focus on the areas most relevant to you.

THE THREE SUBTYPES OF DEPRESSION

Terms like "depression" and "anxiety" are used very broadly today. You may think that the diagnosis of "major depression," for example, refers to a single condition that will respond to a particular treatment. Yet various people labeled with this diagnosis can have dramatic differences in their symptoms, reflecting what is going on with their brain chemistry. It is important to remember that depression is not a single entity, and if you can refine your understanding, then you may be able to find a more direct way out of it.

We find it useful to distinguish among three subtypes of depression:

- *Anxious depression*, where mood is low and there are also strong feelings of anxiety, insecurity, and impulsivity

- *Agitated depression*, where anger or irritability are the predominant moods, often accompanied by physical agitation and sometimes by compulsive behaviors

- *Sluggish depression*, with a dulled or flat mood and strong feelings of lethargy, sleepiness, and lack of motivation

These distinct patterns often reflect very different brain-chemical imbalances. Find out if you are prone to one of these subtypes of depression by taking the following questionnaire.

What Type of Depression Do You Have?

For each question, mark the answer that best describes you. If more than one answer seems to fit, mark both, or all three:

1. My mood is predominantly:

    a. anxious, stressed, or highly changeable.

    b. irritable, agitated, or easily upset.

    c. sad, down, or flat.

2. My mind tends to be:

    a. fearful, scanning for perceived dangers.

    b. filled with judgment or resentments.

    c. dulled, slowed down.

3. Mostly, my physical energy is:

    a. tense, fluctuating, and easily run down.

    b. restless, agitated, and prone to periods of exhaustion.

    c. sluggish and lethargic.

4. I frequently have trouble:

    a. falling asleep, largely due to worry and difficulty shutting down my mind.

    b. staying asleep, as I am easily disturbed and my mind is very restless.

    c. waking up in the morning; I feel like I could sleep most of the time yet never feel rested.

5. I typically react to stress by:

    a. feeling frazzled and overwhelmed.

    b. becoming more "revved up" or angry.

    c. feeling passive or wanting to give up.

6. I usually respond to perceived criticism by:

    a. feeling sensitive or rejected.

  b. becoming defensive or angry.

  c. pulling away or shutting down.

7. In many of my relationships, I have become:

  a. somewhat clinging or dependent.

  b. rather hostile or resentful.

  c. fairly distant or withdrawn.

8. My appetite has recently been:

  a. marked by cravings and binges on sweets and other carbohydrates.

  b. fluctuating with frequent indigestion or stomach upset.

  c. reduced, as I have less interest in food.

9. My motivation seems:

  a. weak, fear based, driven by insecurity.

  b. driven, perhaps with an edge of desperation.

  c. reduced, flat, or apathetic.

10. With regard to pleasure, I tend to be:

  a. impulsively searching for anything to fill the void and make me feel better.

  b. compulsively driven, even addictive, feeling that I've got to have what I desire.

  c. passive, with little interest in or enjoyment of pleasure.

Scoring

Count the number of answers that were:

  a: _____ (corresponds to an anxious type of depression)

  b: _____ (corresponds to an agitated type of depression)

  c: _____ (corresponds to a sluggish type of depression)

Your score can help you decide which set of recommendations below will be most helpful to you. If you scored significantly higher in one category, then begin with recommendations for that type. If you're unsure of your results, it may help to ask someone who knows you well to help you complete the questionnaire. Also, fill out the additional questionnaires later in this chapter on the neurotransmitter imbalances.

Remember that it's possible to have a combined type of depression with high scores in multiple categories. If so, we suggest that you first work on anxiety, then agitation, and finally sluggishness. Or simply begin by working on whichever symptoms are most distressing to you.

THE CHEMICALS OF MOOD

Nerve cells (also called neurons) communicate with one another with the help of chemicals called *neurotransmitters*. There are many such brain chemicals, but when it comes to depression, the big three are serotonin, dopamine, and norepinephrine.

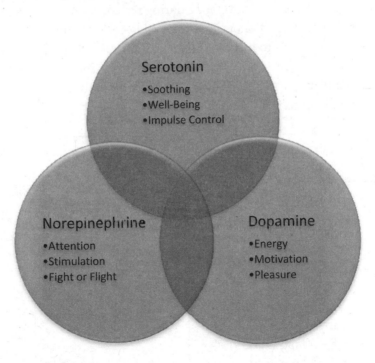

Serotonin could be considered the *well-being chemical*. It has many important functions, including calming the brain, soothing the emotions, and controlling behavioral impulses. When it is deficient, the usual result is anxious depression, though serotonin depletion can be involved in all three types of depression.

Norepinephrine (the *fight-or-flight chemical*) and dopamine (the *pleasure chemical*) work in tandem to provide energy and focus. Together they help keep us alert, motivated, and able to enjoy life's pleasures. It is possible to have either too much or too little of these stimulating brain chemicals, with dramatically different results. In excess they can cause agitated depression, especially if there is too little serotonin to provide a calming balance. Deficiency, on the other hand, often leads to the mental dullness and physical lethargy of sluggish depression.

We will take a closer look at the three subtypes of depression in a moment, but first let's explore a few nutrients that we think are essential for a resilient brain in all of us.

BASIC NUTRITIONAL SUPPORT

We view nutritional supplements as a means of supporting the body's natural functions, helping to correct an imbalance, or replenishing essential elements that may have become depleted. Ideally their use can be temporary until recovery is complete, and then natural food sources can give the brain what it needs to remain healthy and balanced.

There are a few nutrients that provide foundational support for all the subtypes of depression. We recommend the following supplements for everyone during recovery from depression, at times of heightened stress, or when one's diet is less than optimal. The table below outlines the most important brain-healthy nutrients, along with options to minimize their cost. We also list food sources that can help you maintain a good supply of these same nutrients after you have regained your resilience.

All of these supplements are absorbed better if taken with meals, except for the probiotics, which are best taken on an empty stomach.

Supplement	Directions	Less-Expensive Alternatives	Food Sources
Multivitamin with at least 50 mg of B_6 per daily dose	Take half the daily dose with breakfast and half with supper	B complex with at least 50 mg of B_6	Whole grains; dried beans; meat, fish, and dairy; fresh vegetables
Omega-3: fish oil or krill oil	2,000 mg omega-3 (or 1,000 mg of EPA) daily. If needed, increase to 6,000–8,000 mg (or 3,000–4,000 mg of EPA) daily	2 T ground flaxseed or 1 T of flax oil per day.	Fatty fish: salmon, sardines, herring Nuts: walnuts, almonds Seeds: pumpkin, chia, hemp

Vitamin D$_3$	0–2,000 IU daily from April–October 2,000–5,000 IU from October–April (get vitamin D level above 40)	15 minutes of sun exposure 3–4 days per week	Fish, eggs, fortified foods (for example, milk, orange juice, cereals)
Minerals: calcium, magnesium, and zinc	Calcium: 500–1,500 mg daily (women only) Magnesium: 250–750 mg daily Zinc: 15–30 mg daily	A single supplement combining all three	Leafy greens and fruits, dairy, whole grains, nuts and seeds, beans and legumes
Probiotics	2 or more live cultures (for example, lactobacillus and bifidobacterium)	Eat fermented foods several times per week.	Yogurt, kefir, sauerkraut, tempeh, miso, natto, kimchi

The foundational nutrients above may improve your mood on their own, and they will assure that the supplements or medications for each subtype of depression have a much better chance of working. We will now look at these three types one at a time, with additional questionnaires to help you decide if you have a specific neurotransmitter imbalance.

ANXIOUS DEPRESSION

By far the most common subtype of depression, anxious depression has become an epidemic in our times. Serotonin levels are under siege, in part because of our stressful lives, but even more importantly because we react to those stresses in ways that keep the stress hormones elevated. On the other side of the equation, inactive lifestyles and poor diets make it harder to produce adequate amounts of serotonin.

With too little serotonin, even mildly stressful situations can cause your mood to plummet. People with serotonin deficiency often feel insecure, have a hard time putting themselves out into the world, and may feel a need to retreat or withdraw, even from friends. They sometimes try to make themselves feel better through impulsive behaviors like binge eating or alcohol use, or engaging in overly dependent relationships.

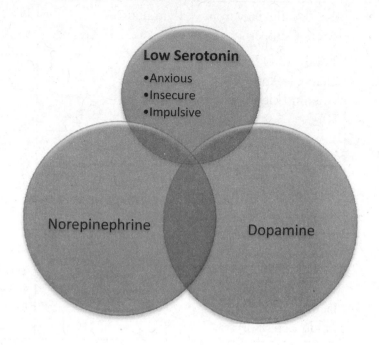

• *Molly's Story*

Molly was a nineteen-year-old college student. Like many people her age, she felt stressed by school pressures and the transition to adulthood. She worried about her mother's depression since her parents' divorce two years ago. Though Molly had friends at school, she felt isolated and withdrawn: "I know it sounds weird, but I can feel alone even when I'm with a bunch of people."

Molly's mood was depressed, but she also felt anxious and insecure. While her energy was poor, both her body and mind were in constant motion. She had trouble falling and staying asleep, and often had anxious or troubling dreams. She felt unable to handle even mild stresses, like having to write papers or take exams. Her symptoms were worse before her periods, when she also became unusually irritable.

Molly had several signs of low serotonin. Her symptoms were mild, so we agreed to start with the serotonin-boosting supplements discussed later in this chapter. She felt so much better after two weeks that medications were not needed. However, she still had problems during the week before her period, so we had her increase her dose of 5-HTP and vitamin B6 for those few days each month. Her PMS symptoms were then 80 percent better.

Do You Have a Serotonin Deficiency?

Mark each of the following statements that describes you at this time (last few days or weeks):

- ☐ My mood is anxious or irritable.
- ☐ I have insomnia.
- ☐ I crave carbohydrates or binge eat.
- ☐ My energy is restless.
- ☐ I have an overactive mind and am easily worried.
- ☐ I have feelings of insecurity.
- ☐ I am often impulsive.
- ☐ I have a low tolerance or overreactivity to stress.
- ☐ I am highly sensitive to criticism or rejection.
- ☐ I have feelings of low self-esteem.
- ☐ I tend to be dependent in relationships.
- ☐ I am sensitive to seasonal changes in the amount of daylight (seasonal affective disorder, or SAD).
- ☐ I have strong emotional challenges with my monthly cycles (premenstrual syndrome).
- ☐ I have had problems with alcohol abuse or a family history of alcoholism.
- ☐ I have chronic pain.

Scoring

Add the total number of items checked.

1–5: mild serotonin deficiency

6–10: moderate serotonin deficiency

11–15: severe serotonin deficiency

Remember that this is not *you*. It only describes you at this moment in time, and you can change it by supporting your brain chemistry with the calming supplement program that follows, and by following all of the pathways to joy.

Natural Therapies to Calm an Anxious Depression

If you have mild to moderate symptoms of anxious depression, especially if you appear to have a serotonin deficiency, you may find it helpful to add one or more of the following supplements. They are listed roughly in order of their usefulness, so start with the first supplement and add the others only if you don't feel better within three to four weeks.

5-HTP (5-hydroxytryptophan): Start with 50 mg twice daily (on an empty stomach if tolerated). If there's no response, you may increase the dosage by 50 mg every three to four days, up to 300 mg daily if needed.

Tryptophan is an amino acid found in food that gets converted first into 5-HTP and then into serotonin. Both tryptophan and 5-HTP can raise serotonin levels in the brain (Nadia et al. 2011), improving mood, sleep, and memory (Silber and Schmitt 2010). Whereas tryptophan is more sedating and used mainly for sleep, 5-HTP can be either mildly stimulating or sedating.

It is best to take 5-HTP on an *empty* stomach, about thirty minutes before or a couple of hours after meals. If it causes mild nausea or headache, it may be taken with food. There must be plenty of B vitamins (especially B6), magnesium, and vitamin C to aid in the process of serotonin production, so keep your foundational nutrition strong.

Note that 5-HTP should not be taken with an antidepressant without medical supervision. It can be dangerous to get too much serotonin. Signs of excess serotonin include sweating, muscle cramps, agitation, or restlessness.

St. John's wort: 300 mg two or three times daily with meals (may increase by 300 mg every two to three weeks, up to 1,500 mg daily). It should be standardized to 0.3 percent hypericum or 5 percent hyperforin.

This herbal therapy has long been used to treat depression. It is often considered less effective for *severe* depression (Davidson et al. 2002), but researchers have concluded that St. John's wort *is* helpful for mild to moderate depression, especially with anxiety (Linde, Berner, and Kriston 2009). Side effects are mild, and can include slight sedation, restlessness, or nausea. St. John's wort may interfere with certain medications, including psychotropic drugs and birth control pills, so be sure to tell your doctor if you are taking it.

Do not take for bipolar depression or add to an antidepressant without medical supervision.

Passionflower: 1 to 2 capsules (or 10 to 20 drops) up to three or four times per day as needed for anxiety.

Passionflower is a gently calming herb, shown to be as effective for anxiety as a potent antianxiety drug, but with far fewer side effects (Akhondzadeh et al. 2001). It may not lift mood directly, but passionflower can provide much-needed calm during the storm of anxious depression. It may be used just occasionally, but if anxiety is persistent, it can be taken three or four times daily for up to several weeks.

AGITATED DEPRESSION

Though it is less common than anxious depression, an increasing number of people suffer from depression characterized by states of agitation and irritability. Perhaps this is due to nonstop stress and fast-paced lifestyles, along with the stimulants used to fuel them: caffeine, energy drinks, sweeteners (either sugar or artificial), and drugs of all types. At the same time, many people haven't the time or the ability to soothe themselves when they feel upset or overwhelmed.

Agitation can be easily overlooked because people usually describe their moods as simply "depressed." A closer look, however, will show that instead of sadness, there is a degree of edginess to their moods. When they say they feel "bad," that means they feel angry, irritable, or aggressive. Their brains are on overdrive from the internal stimulants norepinephrine and dopamine.

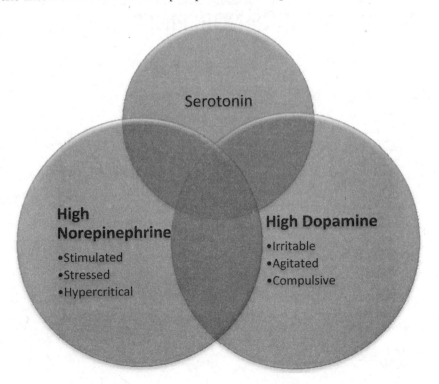

- ## *Josh's Story*

"I'm depressed and I can't sleep. My doctor put me on Prozac and I felt much worse!"

Josh is a forty-two-year-old executive on the fast track. Always driven, he had become compulsive about both work and exercise. He put in twelve- to fourteen-hour days, got up at 4:30 a.m. to exercise, and fueled himself with a high-protein diet and tons of caffeine. Josh was depressed, but he was also physically restless, cranky with his kids, and critical of nearly everyone. He couldn't sleep because his mind could not settle down. Faced with a failing marriage and negative feedback at work, he finally gave in to friends' suggestions that he get help.

His first move was to get on Prozac. Like many people with agitated depression, Josh had a paradoxical reaction—the medication made him feel more agitated and moody. That scared him enough that he was willing to make some significant lifestyle changes. He curbed his caffeine and scheduled downtime for himself and quality time with his family. He added the soothing supplements below, with a special focus on his sleep.

His anxiety and irritability improved greatly. He was still depressed, however, so we added a very low dose of a less stimulating serotonin drug—just 10 mg of citalopram. He only needed it for a few months, and could then sustain his mood through lifestyle changes and supplements.

DO YOU HAVE A DOPAMINE-NOREPINEPHRINE EXCESS?

Mark each of the following statements that describes you at this time:

- ☐ My mood is angry or irritable.

- ☐ I have insomnia.

- ☐ I have acid indigestion.

- ☐ My energy is restless and excessive, but at times I may feel extremely fatigued.

- ☐ I have an overactive mind and am easily agitated.

- ☐ I have feelings of hostility.

- ☐ I am often driven or compulsive.

- ☐ I typically overreact to stress by becoming more upset or ill-tempered.

- ☐ I easily become critical or rejecting.

- ☐ I am usually unaware of feelings of low self-esteem.

- ☐ I tend to be rejecting in relationships.

☐ I am sensitive to changes in light, often feeling more wired or restless in spring or summer.

☐ I have strong emotional challenges with my monthly cycles (premenstrual syndrome).

☐ I have had problems with drug abuse or a family history of alcoholism or drug abuse.

☐ I have high blood pressure.

Scoring

Add the total number of items checked.

1–5: mild dopamine-norepinephrine excess

6–10: moderate dopamine-norepinephrine excess

11–15: severe dopamine-norepinephrine excess

Remember that this is only a reflection of your current brain chemistry, and you can rebalance using the soothing supplement program below and by following all of the pathways to joy.

Natural Therapies to Soothe Agitated Depression

If your scores suggest a norepinephrine-dopamine excess, or if you have signs of an agitated depression, the following supplements may help bring you back into balance. Start with the first supplement listed and add the others only if you don't feel better within three to four weeks.

L-theanine: 100–200 mg twice daily. The key to recovering from agitated depression is to focus on calming the brain. L-theanine is an amino acid that helps regulate dopamine and norepinephrine and also supports the key role of GABA, the brain's primary calming chemical (Nathan et al. 2006). L-theanine can improve attentiveness while calming brain activity and soothing agitated emotions. It is well tolerated, but if you feel sedated or fuzzy-headed, you could take it just at bedtime.

5-HTP: 50–100 mg up to three times daily. Boosting serotonin levels can also soothe agitation, so adding 5-HTP can be helpful here as well as with anxious depressions. Start with 50 mg daily and increase gradually, by 50 mg every three to four days. Be careful that agitation does not get worse (as often happens with SSRI medications).

Do not take 5-HTP with a medication without your doctor's supervision.

NAC: 600–1,200 mg twice daily. N-acetyl cysteine (NAC) is an amino acid that is converted into glutathione, a potent antioxidant in the brain. It has a calming effect, and when added to other remedies (including medications), it can help relieve depression (Berk et al. 2008). NAC is considered quite safe, and causes very few side effects except for occasional nausea, constipation, or loose stools.

SLUGGISH DEPRESSION

This pattern of depression can occur at any time, but it is more common in winter, when the body thinks it is time to hibernate. It can also be the end result of prolonged stress or other types of depression if they lead to a state of depletion in the brain chemicals that keep you energized and motivated: dopamine and norepinephrine.

Many people picture this pattern when they think of "clinical depression," in part because the symptoms make it hard to hide sluggish depression. Mood is often described as sad, down, or simply dulled. Both mind and body seem to move slowly, as if shrouded by fog or carrying an extra-heavy burden. Sleep (as much as twelve to fourteen hours a day) is often seen as a welcome escape but is seldom restoring. It is common to lose interest in normal pursuits and find little pleasure in anything.

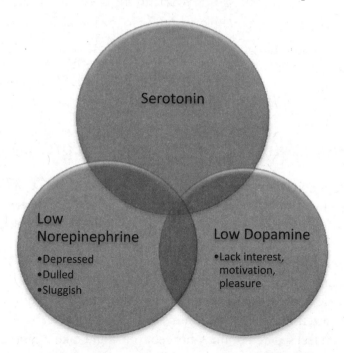

- *Joanne's Story*

Joanne is in her mid-fifties and married with two grown children. She has always struggled with weight, adding a few pounds each winter, and even more so with menopause.

Her mood always drops in winter, too, and she no longer recovers fully over the summers. Twelve years ago she went on Zoloft, which helped dramatically at first, but its benefits have faded over the years. The dose kept getting increased, plus a stimulant was added for energy and a sedative for sleep—and she still felt miserable. Her mood became flat, she felt lifeless, and she could barely get herself up and ready for the day. She slept ten to twelve hours per night, yet never felt rested. She knew that she should exercise and eat better, but couldn't muster up the motivation to do either.

Joanne had sluggish depression with a seasonal pattern. Medications helped at first but gradually failed her, and in the end they seemed to add to her fatigue, weight gain, and even her depressed mood. She gradually cut back on her medication as the basic and energizing supplements discussed later in this chapter helped get them working again. As she felt better, she began to exercise and eat a lighter diet. By the following spring, she was able to get off the medications entirely, and now uses only low doses for a few months each winter.

Do You Have a Norepinephrine or Dopamine Deficiency?

Mark each of the following statements that describes you at this time:

- ☐ My mood is flat or depressed.

- ☐ I have trouble getting out of bed in the morning and tend to sleep too much.

- ☐ I easily put on weight even when I don't binge eat.

- ☐ My energy is lethargic.

- ☐ I have a sluggish mind and am often inattentive.

- ☐ I have feelings of apathy and passivity.

- ☐ I may not like feeling stressed, but am slow to take action to change things.

- ☐ I am sensitive to criticism or rejection, and tend to turn inward as a result.

- ☐ I have feelings of low self-esteem, further causing me to withdraw.

- ☐ I tend to be isolated, with few supportive relationships.

- ☐ I am sensitive to changes in light, becoming excessively tired with drastic changes in sleep patterns in winter.

- ☐ I have low sex drive, or I've had problems with impotence.

- ☐ I have poor memory.

☐   I have little interest in, and derive little enjoyment from, my usual activities.

☐   If I have any addictions, they tend to involve nicotine, caffeine, or stimulant drugs.

Scoring

Add the total number of items checked.

1–5: mild dopamine-norepinephrine deficiency

6–10: moderate dopamine-norepinephrine deficiency

11–15: severe dopamine-norepinephrine deficiency

Remember that this is not permanent, but simply a reflection of how you are at this time. You can become reenergized using the supplement program below and by following all of the pathways to joy.

Natural Therapies to Energize Sluggish Depression

If you have a norepinephrine-dopamine deficiency, or feel sluggish and lethargic when you become depressed, consider the following supplements. You may wish to begin with SAM-e, usually the most potent of these supplements, and then add the others only if you don't improve within two to three weeks.

SAM-e: 400-1,600 mg daily. Take it about thirty minutes before breakfast and/or lunch. S-adenosyl methionine (SAM-e) supports the production of several key hormones and chemicals, including serotonin, norepinephrine, and dopamine (Williams et al. 2005). It has been shown to relieve depression even if prescription antidepressants have failed (Alpert et al. 2004).

SAM-e works quickly and can be quite energizing, so start low (400 mg daily) and increase no sooner than once a week and no higher than 1,600 mg daily. If you take more than 800 mg daily, it is best to split it into two doses (before breakfast and lunch).

SAM-e has been known to trigger a manic episode in people with bipolar disorder, and should not be added to medications without your doctor's supervision.

L-tyrosine and/or DL-phenylalanine: 500–1,500 mg daily. Tyrosine and phenylalanine are the amino acid building blocks for dopamine and norepinephrine respectively, and mood can become depressed if they are deficient (Ruhé, Mason, and Schene 2007). Taken as supplements, these amino acid precursors can give a boost to mood, motivation, and energy (Lakhan and Vieira 2008). Start with either of them at 500 mg daily, and increase by 500 mg once a week if necessary. The two may be combined with one another, or even with 5-HTP if there are also signs of serotonin deficiency. They can be stimulating, so watch for problems with anxiety, agitation, or insomnia.

Be careful if you have hypertension; these supplements can elevate blood pressure.

Chromium: 200–500 mcg daily. Chromium is a mineral that assists with cellular energy production and can also stabilize blood sugar (Albarracin et al. 2008). It may be helpful for sluggish depression, especially with carbohydrate craving or binge eating (Davidson et al. 2003). When used in the amounts listed, chromium is considered safe, with few possible side effects including mild headache or nausea.

HOW TO USE MEDICATION WISELY

Natural therapies are not always effective enough on their own to treat or prevent depression. Prescription antidepressants are far from perfect, but they can be helpful and occasionally even life saving. If you need medication to help in your recovery, please don't see this as a failure or a sign of weakness. It is simply another option to be called upon when needed.

Antidepressant medications fall into two categories: before Prozac and after Prozac. The older drugs (the tricyclic antidepressants and MAO inhibitors) are seldom used today, in part because they have many side effects and pose other risks.

Introduced in 1987, Prozac changed everything about the treatment of depression. It was the first of the *selective serotonin reuptake inhibitors* (SSRIs), a class that includes other well-known drugs like Zoloft, Paxil, Celexa, and Lexapro. Since they work through the serotonin system, the SSRIs are most helpful with anxious depression, but can also be used with agitated or sluggish depression. Considered safer and easier to tolerate, they are used much more freely than the older drugs. But they are not without their problems.

The term "reuptake inhibitor" means that after serotonin has been released into the gap between nerve cells, these drugs prevent its reuptake back into the neuron where it could be stored and used again later. That keeps the serotonin molecule in the synapse longer, where it continues its important job of communicating with other neurons. Remember, though, that there is really no more serotonin than before; it just seems that way. Since the SSRIs prevent the recycling of serotonin, they can lead to even further serotonin depletion if you aren't careful. That's another reason why we put so much emphasis on exercise, diet, and nutritional supplements; they can create *lasting* conditions for a healthy brain.

Another category of antidepressants is known as *serotonin and norepinephrine reuptake inhibitors* (SNRIs). Since they work on both types of brain chemicals, they can be both calming (especially at low doses) and energizing (especially at moderate to high doses). Effexor, Cymbalta, and Pristiq may be good choices for a sluggish type of depression, or for any depression that has been severe or long lasting, or has not gotten better with other measures.

Bupropion (Wellbutrin) is the only antidepressant that works mostly through dopamine. It is usually stimulating, which can be good for sluggish or winter depressions, but can also trigger anxiety, agitation, or insomnia, especially if the dose is too high.

Besides the antidepressants, there are three other classes of drugs that are often used to help in the treatment of depression:

- *Antianxiety drugs* like lorazepam (Ativan), alprazolam (Xanax), and clonazepam (Klonopin) are effective at calming anxiety but can be sedating and are habit forming if used for more than a few weeks.

- *Antipsychotic medications* (including Seroquel, Geodon, Zyprexa, and Abilify) block the effects of dopamine and can reduce agitation and mood swings. Since they have potentially serious side effects, such as metabolic and movement problems, we suggest that they be used for depression at very low doses for short periods of time.

- *Mood stabilizers* such as lamotrigine (Lamictal) or gabapentin (Neurontin) calm brain activity, so they can be used in very low doses for anxiety, or in moderate doses for agitation.

The decision to take medication is best made by you with input from your doctor, therapist, and family. Here are a few guidelines that may make medications as helpful and problem free as possible.

How Do You Know If You Need Medications?

Consider taking medications if you have any of the following symptoms:

- Severe depression that makes it hard to function in daily life, or is accompanied by suicidal or self-destructive thoughts

- Moderate depression that has not improved within three to four weeks of trying natural therapies

- Mild depression that has not improved within six to eight weeks of trying natural therapies

- A severe sleep disturbance that does not improve with natural therapies

- Repeated episodes of depression, especially if they occur without any particular trigger or stressor

The Right Medication and How Much to Take

The following suggestions about medications for each of the subtypes of depression are based upon our clinical experience. In general, you should take the lowest dose needed to improve symptoms. With mild to moderate depression, try to stay within the low-dose ranges as long as possible, preferably for at least three to six weeks to give the medications a chance to work. If there is little improvement within that time, the dose may need to be increased to the moderate range. With severe depression, the dose may need to be increased more quickly.

Sometimes it is necessary to use higher doses than those listed, but side effects then become much more common. The basic supplements (mentioned earlier) may help medications remain effective at the lowest possible dose.

Remember that many people who go on medications just need temporary support and can then transition to other means of staying healthy, like those suggested throughout this workbook.

Medication Support for Anxious Depression

Medications for Anxious Depression	Low Daily Dose Range for Anxiety	Comments
fluoxetine (Prozac)	10–20 mg	Jitteriness, insomnia, or agitation may make Prozac less favorable for anxiety.
sertraline (Zoloft)	25–50 mg	Helpful for anxiety; side effects are weight gain and sedation.
paroxetine (Paxil)	10–20 mg	Weight gain, sedation, and intense withdrawal problems make it less favorable.
citalopram (Celexa)	10–20 mg	Good choice for anxiety; can be sedating.
escitalopram (Lexapro)	5–10 mg	Good choice for anxiety; very similar to citalopram but usually better tolerated.
venlafaxine (Effexor)	37.5–75 mg	Dose needs to be quite low or it can be stimulating.
duloxetine (Cymbalta)	20–30 mg	Dose needs to be quite low or it can be stimulating.
gabapentin (Neurontin)	100–300 mg twice daily	Calming but can occasionally depress mood.

KEYS TO RECOVERY FROM ANXIOUS DEPRESSION

- Focus on calming medications (those affecting serotonin or GABA).

- Keep doses low if possible. Be patient, allowing plenty of time for lower doses to work.

- Reducing stresses and improving sleep will lead to quicker recovery.

- Try to keep medication use short term (three to nine months) and focus on stress reduction.

Medication Support for Agitated Depression

Medications for Agitated Depression	Low Daily Dose Range for Agitation	Comments
SSRIs: Zoloft, Celexa, Lexapro	Same as with anxious depression	Any SSRI can worsen agitation (especially Prozac and Paxil), so the initial dose should be very low and increases very gradual.
quetiapine (Seroquel)	10–50 mg at bedtime	Can be quite sedating; watch weight gain; best if used only when needed.
aripiprazole (Abilify)	2–5 mg, can be used during the day	Less sedation and weight gain but still carries risks. Can be quite helpful for agitation but still best kept short term.
lamotrigine (Lamictal)	100–200 mg	May stabilize mood; usually well tolerated, it may be safely used longer term.

KEYS TO RECOVERY FROM AGITATED DEPRESSION

- Focus on soothing medications (those boosting serotonin or reducing dopamine).

- Keep doses as low as possible, especially at the start. Be very careful that agitation or mood swings do not worsen.

- Reducing stimulation and improving sleep will lead to quicker recovery.

- Try to keep medication use as short as possible, unless mood is clearly more stable on medication.

Medication Support for Sluggish Depression

Medications for Sluggish Depression	Moderate Daily Dose Range for Lethargy	Comments
SSRI (Prozac)	20–40 mg	Prozac is the most stimulating SSRI; at higher doses, all SSRIs can suppress (flatten) mood.
Effexor	75–225 mg	Gets more stimulating as dose is increased; watch blood pressure and sleep.
Cymbalta	30–60 mg	May also be more stimulating as dose gets higher.
desvenlafaxine (Pristiq)	50 mg	Similar to Effexor but may be better tolerated.
bupropion (Wellbutrin)	150–300 mg	One of the most stimulating antidepressants. May be added to an SSRI, especially during winter months. Seems easier to come off than most meds, especially if exercising regularly.

KEYS TO RECOVERY FROM SLUGGISH DEPRESSION

- Focus on energizing medications (those affecting norepinephrine or dopamine).

- Moderate doses may be needed and are typically well tolerated.

- Increasing activity (especially vigorous exercise) and moderating sleep (to seven to nine hours) will keep recovery going.

- Medications may be needed longer with this type. With seasonal depression, you may be able to stop medications during the summer months and resume the next fall if needed.

When to Stop Your Medications, and How

Be sure to follow your doctor's advice as to when and how to come off medications. If you have suffered from severe depression or if it has been recurrent, you may need to stay on them longer than the ranges given above.

It is easiest to get off medications if you have been on them for just a few months. Even so, there can be withdrawal symptoms ranging from mild physical problems (including dizziness, fatigue, headache, or nausea) to intense psychological symptoms (such as feeling even more anxious or depressed than before taking medication). Try to choose a time that is optimal for you to go through any such difficulty. Most people do best coming off medications in the spring and summer, and when life is not overly stressful. If you still develop difficult withdrawal symptoms, slow it down and let yourself stabilize before making another dose reduction, and always do this with your doctor's supervision.

SUMMING UP CHAPTER 4

- Depression comes in different forms, and understanding your own pattern can help you choose the most helpful remedies.

- You can identify safe and effective natural means to balance your brain chemistry and support your mood.

- When medications are needed, choose the right medication for your type of depression, take the lowest effective dose, and stay on it only as long as necessary.

Chapter 5

Flowing:

Live in Rhythm with Your Nature

It is in…a profound instinctive union with the stream of life that the greatest joy is to be found.

Bertrand Russell

"**I**'ve been so edgy and irritable lately. Something is not right, but I can't put my finger on it. This just doesn't feel like me."

Sarah is describing an experience common to us all. In its early stages, this may be nothing more than a minor imbalance, easily corrected. But if it continues, such an imbalance may lead to one of the subtypes of depression described in the last chapter.

If at all possible, it is best to prevent depression before it takes hold by staying balanced and feeling like *you*. This includes knowing and accepting your own nature and creating a lifestyle that promotes it. To support this goal, this chapter will help you to do the following.

- Identify your natural mind-body type.

- Learn to recognize early signs of mind-body imbalance.

- Identify simple and effective measures to regain balance and sustain it long term.

Joyful living is dynamic and ever changing; it involves being in a state of flow, in union with the stream of life and with the natural world. Yet each person is unique, and what is healing for you may not be for someone else. When it comes to maintaining vibrant health, one size does not fit all. We have to live in harmony with our own nature.

Know Yourself: Discover Your Natural Mind-Body Type

There is a great deal of conflicting advice about basic lifestyle measures, making it hard to know what is best for *you*. We all need good sleep, for example, but how do you know how much sleep your own body needs to function at its best? Eating a healthy, natural diet will help everyone feel better. But does it really make sense that the same diet is suited for everyone?

The following questionnaire will help you discover your *natural* state, the physical and mental tendencies you have had most of your life. Knowing this will help you make your best diet and lifestyle choices.

For each question, mark the answer that best describes you *as you typically are* (the way you've been for most of your life). If more than one answer seems to fit, mark two or all three. For greater accuracy, you may want to ask someone who has known you for a long time to help fill out your answers.

1. My natural body type is:

    a. light and narrow-framed with prominent joints; if I gain weight, it tends to be in the midsection.

    b. medium build, athletic, moderate weight; I can gain or lose weight easily if I put my mind to it.

    c. sturdy and large-boned; I gain weight easily and have trouble taking it off again.

2. My skin tends to be:

    a. cold, dry, or rough, especially in dry climates.

    b. warm and burn easily, and I tend to have freckles, moles, or rashes.

    c. cool, soft, and oily.

3. I prefer a climate that is:

   a. warm and moist; I don't tolerate dry, cold winds.

   b. cool and dry; I don't tolerate hot, humid weather.

   c. warm and dry; I don't tolerate cool and damp weather.

4. My hair tends to be:

   a. dry, frizzy, and brittle.

   b. straight, light, or reddish, with early balding or graying.

   c. thick, wavy, dark, oily.

5. My appetite tends to be:

   a. variable and irregular; I often skip meals because of my erratic schedule.

   b. strong and occasionally excessive; I get crabby if I miss a meal.

   c. slow and steady; I can go a long time without eating, though I prefer not to.

6. My digestion tends to be:

   a. irregular, with frequent gas or constipation.

   b. quick, with occasional burning indigestion or loose stools.

   c. slow and sluggish, often with oily stools.

7. Physically, I tend to be:

   a. highly active, moving quickly; sometimes I get restless.

   b. medium active, moving purposefully; sometimes I become driven to get things done.

   c. lower in activity, moving slowly and methodically; sometimes I get lethargic.

8. My mind is best described as:

   a. quick, active, restless; I am quick to learn new things.

   b. sharp, intelligent, critical; I am determined to learn things well.

   c. calm, slow, thoughtful; I learn slowly and steadily.

9. My memory is usually:

    a. quick to remember, but also quick to forget.

    b. strong and distinct.

    c. slow to develop but with good retention.

10. My sleep is usually:

    a. irregular and light, and I am easily awakened.

    b. fairly sound, and I need less than average to feel rested.

    c. deep and heavy, and I need more than average to feel rested.

11. When I feel like myself, I tend to be:

    a. lively, creative, and enthusiastic; I embrace change.

    b. determined, friendly, and successful; I embrace competition.

    c. calm, easygoing, and nurturing; I embrace structure.

12. When I feel stressed, I tend to become:

    a. anxious, insecure, or moody.

    b. agitated, irritable, or impatient.

    c. sluggish, complacent, or withdrawn.

Scoring

Count the number of answers that were:

    a: _____ (corresponds to the air type)

    b: _____ (corresponds to the fire type)

    c: _____ (corresponds to the earth type)

If your score in one category is significantly higher than in the others, then that is your mind-body type. However, most people score high in two categories (one is often slightly higher than the other) and are a two-part combination type. Rarely, the scores are nearly equal in all three categories (a three-part combination type).

Understanding Your Scores

The preceding questionnaire is adapted from ayurveda, the traditional medicine from India. You don't need to know ayurvedic medicine in detail to make good use of this information. You will simply use this as a guide for making self-care choices that are best for *you*.

If you had more "a" answers, then you are likely to be lively, creative, enthusiastic—and constantly changing. When you become stressed, however, your emotions may tend toward fear and anxiety, and you could become susceptible to anxious depression. This pattern is referred to as the *air type*.

If you had more "b" answers, then you are likely to be passionate, confident, purposeful—and relentlessly determined. When you become stressed, your emotions may tend toward anger and irritability, leaving you susceptible to agitated depression. We call this pattern the *fire type*.

If you had more "c" answers, then you are likely to be calm, stable, easygoing—and reliably loyal. Your emotions under stress tend toward heaviness and dullness, making you more susceptible to sluggish depression. This pattern is referred to as the *earth type*.

Each of us possesses some of each of these patterns, but in different proportions. It is important to remember that no mind-body type is better than another; they are just different.

It doesn't matter how you compare to others. What is important is to be as true to your own nature as you can be. If you live in harmony with your own nature, then you are more likely to enjoy vibrant health and a peaceful mind. Living out of sync with who you are can open the door to illnesses such as depression.

WHEN YOU'RE OUT OF BALANCE: REALIGN

Staying in balance is an art. When you have balance, you feel good and wonder why you don't *always* feel this way! But despite our best efforts, we all lose that sense of rightness from time to time. The key is to notice that it's gone and immediately do what we can to get back into alignment.

Anyone can experience imbalance in any category, or even all three at once. But if you already have a clear tendency toward one of the three patterns above, then it is easier for that pattern to become imbalanced. Air types, for example, are notorious for keeping irregular schedules, which only furthers their imbalance. Fire types who become too competitive or earth types who are inactive will likewise find that those patterns become exaggerated. Look back at your scores; the categories with the highest scores are those most likely to get out of balance for you.

The three primary patterns are outlined next, along with the key diet and lifestyle choices that will help you regain and then stay in balance. If it is clear where your imbalance lies, you may want to go right to that section. If you are unsure where to begin, then work on the three patterns in order: balance air first, then fire, and finally earth.

After you have regained a greater sense of well-being, then continue with the measures that are best suited for your own mind-body type.

Realigning Air Types

When air types are imbalanced, it may show up in the following ways:

Physical	Mental/Emotional
Dry skin or cracked lips	Feeling worried, restless, and fearful
Irregular appetite	Feeling easily overwhelmed or inadequate
Craving sweets, carbs	Impulsiveness
Bloating, gas, or constipation	Scattered or distracted thinking
Trouble falling asleep, restless sleep	Frenetic activity, unable to slow down

These can be early warning signs of anxious depression. If you take measures to bring yourself back into balance quickly, you may be able to prevent it from going any further.

Discover the Causes of Air Imbalance

Check each of the following statements that applies to you:

☐ I work long or irregular hours.

☐ I don't take regular breaks.

☐ I tend to overschedule myself; my schedule is inconsistent.

☐ I don't get enough sleep.

☐ I use caffeine or nicotine.

☐ I eat a lot of sugar or white flour.

☐ I skip breakfast or other meals.

☐ There is a lot of noise or hustle and bustle around me.

☐ There is a lot of stress or change in my life right now.

☐ I live in a cold, dry climate (or it is winter).

Go over all the items that you checked and deal with any that are within your power to change. The most common causes of imbalance are stress, excessive use of stimulants, and ignoring the need for adequate rest. You will find more on dealing with stress in part 3. Meanwhile, the following are simple, commonsense measures that anyone can take to help bring air energy back into balance.

Seven Guidelines for Balancing Air

Live calmly through the day. A regular routine is essential. Aim to get up and go to bed at the same time each day. Eat meals at regular times, and never skip meals. Try to keep work hours consistent and moderate. Take regular breaks, ideally every one and a half to two hours. Doing nothing once in a while may be your most productive use of time.

Remember to regularly set aside extensive time for reflection and renewal.

Eat wisely for your type. Food should bring warmth, moisture, and substance to return air types to balance; think "comfort food," including warm soups and stews. Minimize dry foods (crackers, cereals) or uncooked foods (raw vegetables). Keep regular mealtimes, with the midday meal being the largest, if possible. Eat slowly and take a few minutes to relax after the meal. Drink warm water throughout the day. Use the list below to guide your food choices.

AIR BALANCING FOODS:

Overview: Modest protein, warm foods with plenty of complex carbohydrates

RECOMMENDED FOODS:

Dairy: Milk and cheese

Meats: Turkey, chicken, seafood

Beans and legumes: Soy, lentils, chickpeas (these may cause gas if you don't have strong digestion)

Nuts and seeds: Almonds and almond butter, sesame seeds and tahini, flaxseeds

Grains: Rice, wheat, oats, amaranth, quinoa, whole-grain breads, hot cereals

Root vegetables: Carrots, onions, beets, radishes, turnips, sweet potatoes, squash

Cooked vegetables: Asparagus, leafy greens, green beans, okra, garlic

Fruits: Sweet, ripe fruits such as grapes, melons, oranges, mangoes, berries, cherries, dates, figs, pineapples, plums, nectarines, bananas

Snacks: Nuts or seeds, fruits, milk or yogurt

Herbs and spices: Anise, basil, cardamom, cinnamon, fennel, ginger, licorice, nutmeg, thyme

Move in tune with your body. You do not need to do vigorous exercise to balance air energy; favor instead any type of rhythmic movement such as dance or tai chi.

Ideal exercise: Walking; aim for twenty to thirty minutes, once or twice daily.

Being in nature and with others is a plus. Consider biking, rowing, hiking, skiing, or dancing.

Best mind-body exercises: Restorative or gentle yoga, or chi gong.

A recent study (Mota-Pereira et al. 2011) used walking to assess the effect of moderate exercise on treatment-resistant depression (depression lasting at least nine months and not responding to two different antidepressant medications). Those in the intervention group were asked to walk for thirty to forty-five minutes per day, five days a week. That group improved in all measures of depression, 50 percent were significantly improved, and one out of four reached full remission. Not one member of the control group (which did not add exercise) reached remission.

Two interesting side notes to this study are:

- In the intervention group, those who were more heavily medicated were less likely to respond.

- Participants were considered to be in compliance if they did at least 50 percent of the amount of walking expected of them. By those criteria, 91 percent were compliant. The researchers were using the 51 Percent Solution described in chapter 2!

Tuck yourself in properly. Air types almost always need more sleep than they are getting, with potentially serious consequences (see sidebar). Keep regular hours and get to bed early. Set aside thirty to forty-five minutes for a relaxed bedtime routine, much as a wise parent does for a child. Set the lights low, turn off the computer or TV, read a story, or take a warm bath. If you like, have a cup of warm milk with a little cardamom or nutmeg.

Avoid alcohol before bed; it may seem to relax you but can further disrupt your sleep.

Researchers focusing on seventeen- to twenty-four-year-olds who were not getting enough sleep found that this was a risk factor for persistent psychological stress. Following nearly three thousand young people for twelve to eighteen months, they discovered that for each hour of lost sleep, levels of psychological stress rose by 5 percent. Those getting the least amount of sleep were 14 percent more likely to report symptoms of psychological stress. If they were already suffering from anxiety, the lack of sleep often led to depression. Even if they were not anxious to begin with, those who slept less than five hours per night tripled their odds of becoming psychologically stressed (Glozier et al. 2010).

Come to your senses. The physical sense that is most soothing for air types is touch, and massage is an ideal way to calm yourself when you are stressed or anxious, and also to treat dry skin. Use warm almond or jojoba oil just before your bath or shower and a gentle moisturizer afterward. You may want to add a few drops of a calming essential oil, like lavender or sweet orange. You can also use these as aromatherapy.

Sound is the second most important sense for air types. Listening to soothing, soft music or sounds of nature may quickly balance your mind and body.

Take a deep breath. You can use the following calming breath technique whenever you get anxious or if you have difficulty sleeping.

Calming Breath

Slowly breathe in through your nose to the count of four. Breathe out through your mouth even more slowly—to the count of seven. Some people find it even more calming to make an audible sigh with your out-breath.

Try the yogic alternate nostril breathing, which is highly recommended for air types. As you exhale, place your thumb or forefinger gently over one nostril, forcing you to breathe out through the other. After inhaling through the same nostril, switch sides. Continue alternating from right to left nostril for a few minutes, or until you feel rebalanced and de-stressed.

Change with the seasons. Air energy is aggravated in the fall and winter, when the weather becomes dry, windy, and cold. If you're an air type, you need to stay warm and keep your skin moist with baths, showers, saunas, and steam rooms, and use moisturizing oils and lotions. This is a particularly important time to follow the dietary suggestions mentioned earlier, sticking with favored foods and avoiding foods that are not recommended. When the weather is cold and windy, you need to pay particular attention to maintaining your exercise routines and daily schedule.

Take Action: Create Your Calming Tool Kit

Here are a few simple, self-nurturing activities you can do to calm yourself whenever you notice that you are becoming more frenetic. Choose a few favorites so that you can take quick action to bring yourself back into balance, and add to the list in the space below:

- Take a walk in nature—alone or with a friend.

- Get outdoors and relax in the sun.

- Drink a warm beverage (no caffeine!).

- Eat a small handful of seeds and nuts (and then take a few minutes' break).

- Read an entertaining or inspiring book.

- Go see a light, fun movie.

- Take a warm bath or shower.

- Take a twenty-minute nap.

- Stop everything else and listen to your favorite soft or classical music.

- Get a massage.

- Go to a yoga class.

- Do five to ten minutes of the calming breath or alternate-nostril breathing.

- Take time for prayer or meditation.

_____

_____

_____

_____

_____

Realigning Fire Types

When fire types are imbalanced, it can show up in the following ways:

Physical	Mental/Emotional
Flushed or irritated skin; rashes	Feeling angry, irritable, or impatient
Acid indigestion, "heartburn"	Overly critical or judgmental

Loose stools, diarrhea, or hemorrhoids	Rigidly perfectionistic or controlling
High blood pressure	Competitive or intolerant of others
Agitated sleeper; trouble staying asleep and may awaken early	Compulsive about work; "type A" personality

These can be early warning signs of agitated depression. Begin the rebalancing measures below right away to keep depression from taking hold.

Discover the Causes of Fire Imbalance

Check each of the following statements that applies to you:

- ☐ I work long hours and push to meet deadlines.

- ☐ I tend to become overly focused on tasks.

- ☐ I don't get enough exercise.

- ☐ I use caffeine or nicotine.

- ☐ I eat a lot of hot, spicy, or greasy foods.

- ☐ I often skip meals or overeat.

- ☐ I have very high expectations of myself (and others).

- ☐ I am either unaware of my feelings of anger or resentment, or I don't express them.

- ☐ I have been under intense stress for a long time.

- ☐ I live in a hot, humid climate (or it is summer).

Go over all the items that you checked and change any that you can. The two most common causes of fire imbalance are intense, long-term stress and ignoring the need to express emotions. You will find more on stress and emotion in part 3. Meanwhile, the following are simple, commonsense measures that anyone can take to help bring fire energy back into balance.

Seven Guidelines for Balancing Fire

Live coolly through the day. A regular routine is essential. Aim to get up and go to bed at the same time each day. To reduce problems from stomach acidity, never skip meals or wait until you're extremely hungry before you eat. Eat an early, light supper so that you're not full when you go to bed. If possible, avoid going outdoors or exercising in the heat of the day. Keep work in perspective, maintaining a healthy balance between work and play. Take regular breaks, ideally every one and a half to two hours.

Remember to regularly set aside extensive time for reflection and renewal.

Eat wisely for your type. Food should bring coolness and substance to help bring fire energy back into balance; think "light, summery foods," including plenty of fresh fruits and vegetables. Fire types need only small to moderate amounts of protein, with little if any red meat. Minimize spicy foods like hot peppers or greasy foods, including deep-fried foods. Keep regular mealtimes, with the midday meal being the largest, if possible (and a light meal at supper). Eat moderately, neither fasting nor indulging in large meals. Take time to relax after eating. Drink plenty of room-temperature water (with lemon or lime if you like) throughout the day. Choose your foods from the following list.

FIRE BALANCING FOODS:

Overview: Lighter foods with plenty of fresh fruits and vegetables

RECOMMENDED FOODS:

Dairy: Milk, cream, butter, yogurt, cottage cheese, egg whites

Meats: Smaller servings of chicken, turkey, shrimp

Beans and legumes: Tofu, lentils, garbanzo, small black or red beans

Nuts and seeds: Almonds, pumpkin and sunflower seeds

Oils: Olive, walnut, or coconut oils; ghee (clarified butter)

Grains: Barley, oats, wheat, white rice, amaranth

Vegetables: Tender salad greens, leafy vegetables, asparagus, celery, zucchini, green beans, and peas; cruciferous vegetables (broccoli, cauliflower, cabbage, bok choy, Brussels sprouts)

Avoid nightshades (potatoes, tomatoes, peppers, eggplant). They often cause joint pain in people prone to inflammation.

Fruits: Apples, cherries, grapes, mangoes, melons, oranges, pears, peaches, pineapple, coconut, pomegranates, plums, raisins, all types of berries

Herbs and spices: Cardamom, coriander (cilantro), parsley, basil, mint, cinnamon, cumin, dill, fennel, lemon and lime, peppermint, saffron, turmeric

Move in tune with your body. You need more regular exercise to balance fire energy—but be careful that it doesn't become too competitive.

Ideal exercise: Swimming (or other water sports or winter activities). Whatever you choose, it should be something you enjoy without becoming overly compulsive or competitive. Aim for thirty to forty-five minutes, three to five times per week.

Being in nature (especially near water) and with others is a plus. Consider rowing, light running, biking, skiing, or skating.

Best mind-body exercises: Tai chi, yoga

Tuck yourself in properly. Fire types can often get by with less sleep than others, but when fire energy becomes excessive, they often awaken in the middle of the night (typically between 2:00 and 4:00 a.m.) and may have trouble getting back to sleep. It is important to get to bed early to try to assure a decent night's sleep. Set aside thirty to forty-five minutes for a relaxed bedtime routine, much as a wise parent does for a child. Set the lights low, turn off the computer or TV, read a story or take a cool shower or bath. If you prefer warm baths, do that at least an hour before bed, so that you are cooling as you fall asleep. Also, take time to exercise early in the day (not after dinner). If you like, have a cup of warm milk with a little cardamom or nutmeg before bed.
Avoid alcohol before bed; it may seem to relax you but can further disrupt your sleep.

Come to your senses. The physical sense that is most soothing for fire types is vision. It is especially good to enjoy natural vistas, looking out over a lake, a mountain valley, or a sunset. If those aren't accessible, flowers, paintings, or photographs can engage the senses of fire types.
Massage is also healing, and can be especially good for the sensitive skin of fire types. Use sunflower or coconut oil, both of which are cooling. You may want to add a few drops of a soothing essential oil like mint, rose, or sandalwood. You can also use these scents for aromatherapy, or spray your skin with cooling rose or sandalwood water throughout the day.

Take a deep breath. You can use the calming breath technique (recommended previously for air types) whenever you get agitated or if you wake in the middle of the night.
You might also try the yogic left-nostril breathing. Inhale through the left nostril and exhale through the right, covering the other side with your thumb or forefinger. Continue in this way for a few minutes, or until you feel rebalanced and de-stressed.

Change with the seasons. Fire energy is often aggravated in the summer, when the weather becomes hot and humid. If you're a fire type, you need to stay cool and dry in the summer. Stay out of the hot sun when you can, and protect yourself with loose-fitting clothing, hats and sunglasses, and oils and lotions. This is a particularly important time to follow the dietary suggestions, sticking with favored foods and avoiding foods that are not recommended. When the weather is hot, you may need to reduce your exercise, and at least choose the coolest time of the day for more vigorous activity.

Take Action: Create Your Soothing Tool Kit

Here are a few simple, self-nurturing activities you can do to soothe yourself whenever you notice that you are becoming more agitated. Choose a few favorites so that you can take quick action to bring yourself back into balance, and add to the list in the space below:

- Enjoy time in nature—but stay out of the hot sun.

- Go for a peaceful ten- to fifteen-minute walk.

- Drink some cool water or noncaffeinated tea with a bit of mint, lemon, or lime.

- Snack on yogurt or sweet, ripe fruit.

- Read an entertaining or inspiring book.

- Laugh with a good comedy, a book, or an amusing friend—or just laugh.

- Take a cool shower or bath.

- Take a twenty-minute nap.

- Stop everything else and listen to your favorite soft or classical music.

- Get a light massage.

- Go to a tai chi or yoga class.

- Do five to ten minutes of the calming breath or left-nostril breathing.

- Take time for prayer or meditation.

_____

_____

_____

_____

_____

Realigning Earth Types

When earth types are imbalanced, it can show up in the following ways:

Physical	Mental/Emotional
Oily skin, chest congestion	Feeling dull or apathetic
Emotional eating, weight gain	Become envious of or dependent on others
Craving fatty foods	Inactive and lethargic; sitting on the sidelines
Slow digestion, constipation	Poor concentration and memory
Excessive sleep, trouble getting up	Stuck in a rut, unable to get moving

These can be early warning signs of sluggish depression. Move into action as soon as you can to prevent yourself from getting stuck in depression.

Discover the Causes of Earth Imbalance

Check each of the following statements that applies to you:

- ☐ I am understimulated at work.

- ☐ I don't exercise often.

- ☐ I tend not to schedule much on evenings or weekends.

- ☐ I often sleep during the day.

- ☐ I use alcohol or sedating medications.

- ☐ I eat a lot of fried or heavy foods.

- ☐ I turn to food when I feel bad, usually sweets or snack foods.

- ☐ There is not much activity around me.

- ☐ There is very little change in my life right now.

- ☐ I live in a cool, damp climate (or it is spring).

Go over all the items that you checked and deal quickly with any that you can. The two most common causes of earth imbalance are lack of stimulation and dealing ineffectively with stress by overeating or shutting down emotionally. You will find more on stress and emotions in part 3. Meanwhile, the following are simple, commonsense measures that anyone can take to help bring earth energy back into balance.

Seven Guidelines for Balancing Earth

Live energetically through the day. A regular routine is essential. Aim to go to bed and get up early each day, especially during the long winter nights. Do not skip meals, especially breakfast. Eat an early, light supper so that you're not full when you go to bed.

Look to add stimulation to your life. Accept challenges and seek novelty both in work and in play: new friends, new hobbies, new places to go. Take regular breaks, ideally every one and a half to two hours. Try to exercise nearly every day.

Remember to regularly set aside extensive time for reflection and renewal.

Eat wisely for your type. The simplest diet advice for earth types is this: eat less. Like all aspects of life, food should add variety, interest, and stimulation to help bring earth energy back into balance. Think of the natural world in spring, a time to detoxify and lose the extra winter energy stored as fat. Eat more salads and bitter, leafy greens. Earth types do well as vegetarians. They need to be sure to get good-quality protein. If meat is eaten, it should be lean. Reduce oily foods, getting just a small amount of healthy fats. Even on a low-fat diet, earth types who eat a lot of sugar or grains tend to gain weight, so reduce them if you can (use small amounts of honey or agave syrup for sweeteners). Keep regular mealtimes, with a low-calorie, high-protein breakfast and a light meal at supper. Make your midday meal more substantial, and include a modest amount of healthy fat so that you don't crave fats in the evening. Go for a short walk after eating to add some stimulation. Sip warm water or green tea throughout the day (a bit of caffeine is okay). Avoid iced or cold drinks, which imbalance earth energy. Make your food choices from the list below.

EARTH BALANCING FOODS:

Overview: More protein, light foods with plenty of fresh vegetables. Minimize starches and sugars. Avoid artificial sweeteners; use a small amount of raw honey.

RECOMMENDED FOODS:

Dairy: Skim milk, small amounts of low-fat cheese, cottage cheese, yogurt, or kefir.

Meats: Low-fat meats, poultry, fish.

Beans and legumes: All are fine.

Nuts and seeds: Sunflower and pumpkin seeds.

Oils: Small amounts of olive or walnut oils.

Grains (small amounts): Quinoa, barley, buckwheat, corn, millet, amaranth, oats, rye.

Vegetables: All are okay, but go easy on potatoes, sweet potatoes, and other starchy vegetables. Spring vegetables are best, such as leafy greens, sprouts, and asparagus—also the cruciferous vegetables (broccoli, cauliflower, cabbage, Brussels sprouts, bok choy).

Fruits: Apples, pears, peaches, apricots, cranberries, cherries, all berries, all citrus.

Snacks: Yogurt with nuts; low-fat string cheese; nonfat smoothie with added protein powder.

Herbs and spices: Fresh basil, thyme, parsley, oregano, or mint; black or cayenne pepper, cardamom, celery seeds, cinnamon, cloves, ginger, lemon, mustard, sage.

Move in tune with your body. Earth types need the most regular and vigorous exercise to stay balanced—ideally every day. Since energy and motivation can be a challenge, consider finding a workout partner, taking a class, or hiring a personal trainer.

Ideal exercise: Interval training. With any activity you choose, go slowly for two to three minutes to warm up. Over the next few minutes, increase the intensity until you push nearly as hard as you can—but just for a minute or so. Then back down to a more relaxed pace for a couple of minutes, allowing yourself to recover before ramping up the intensity again for a minute. Repeat this cycle four to five times for a great energy-boosting workout.

Competitive sports can also be a good way to get energy flowing. As your energy returns, aim for forty-five to sixty minutes of exercise most days. You should break a sweat and get your heart rate elevated.

It is also helpful to combine aerobic and weight training. And remember, walking is nearly the perfect exercise!

Being in nature and with others is a plus. Consider adventurous sports like sea kayaking, mountain biking, and rock climbing. Also good are vigorous biking and Nordic skiing.

Best mind-body exercises: Martial arts like karate, tae kwon do, or tai chi; more vigorous forms of yoga, including heated yoga.

Tuck yourself in properly. Earth types tend to sleep too much and often have a difficult time waking up and getting out of bed on time. Daytime naps are also a temptation, but they tend to make you even more sluggish and should be avoided until your energy is back to normal. If you must nap, keep it short (twenty to thirty minutes) and early in the day (between noon and 3:00 p.m.). It is important to get to bed early and then arise early, ideally before sunrise.

Avoid alcohol before bed; it may seem to relax you but can further disrupt your sleep.

Come to your senses. The physical senses that are most soothing for earth energy are taste and smell (which may partly explain the tendency toward weight gain). Rather than going for quantity, seek out stimulating flavors and aromas. Try a new cuisine or add a variety of interesting spices to your food.

Massage is also healing, and it can be especially good to get a vigorous rubdown or a deep, invigorating massage. Use corn or calamus oil, both of which are invigorating; or get a dry massage, using a silk glove to stimulate the skin and the lymphatic system. You may want to add a few drops of a stimulating essential oil like jasmine, ylang ylang, citrus, or lavender. You can also use these for aromatherapy, stimulating your sense of smell throughout the day. If you are congested, use eucalyptus.

Take a deep breath. You can use the energizing breath technique whenever you get sluggish or have difficulty waking.

Energizing Breath

Breathe in and out through your nose as fast as you can, as if your chest were a bellows. Make the in-breath and out-breath equal in length. Do this for twenty to thirty seconds at first, working up to a minute or two. Stop and slow your breathing if you feel light-headed.

You might also try the yogic right-nostril breathing. Inhale through the right nostril and exhale through the left, covering the other side with your thumb or forefinger. Continue breathing in this way for a few minutes, until you feel rebalanced and energized.

Change with the seasons. Earth energy is often aggravated in the spring, when the weather becomes cool and damp. If you're an earth type, you need to stay warm and dry in the spring.

Winter and early spring are also the times when seasonal depression occurs, and it usually shows up as sluggish depression. Keeping your earth energy balanced may help you avoid this. In addition to all the other recommendations, you may want to add bright-light therapy. The idea is to trick your body into thinking that the days are longer, with an earlier sunrise and a later sunset. So you want to use the light early and/or late in the day. Since most people have a hard time getting up in the morning, the most important time for light exposure is between 7:00 and 9:00 a.m. If you find that you become really sleepy and sluggish in the evening, you may also want to use your light for twenty to thirty minutes in the late afternoon (between 5:00 and 7:00 p.m.). For more details about proper use of light therapy, and for information about recommended products, go to www.partnersinresilience.com.

Take Action: Create Your Energizing Tool Kit

Here are a few simple, self-nurturing activities you can take to calm yourself whenever you notice that you are becoming more sluggish. Choose a few favorites so that you can take quick action to bring yourself back into balance, and add to the list in the space that follows:

- Enjoy time in nature, soaking up the sun, sights, and sounds.

- Go for a brisk fifteen- to twenty-minute walk.

- Drink a warm cup of green or black tea, or an herbal tea with ginger or ginseng.

- Snack on low-fat cheese, nuts, or other high-protein foods.

- Enjoy an action-packed or dramatic book or movie.

- Laugh with a good comedy, a book, or an amusing friend—or just laugh.

- Take a warm shower or bath.

- Go dancing with friends.

- Listen to some lively, energetic music.

- Get a vigorous massage.

- Go to an aerobics or heated yoga class.

- Do five to ten minutes of the energizing breath or right-nostril breathing.

- Take time for prayer or meditation.

_____

_____

_____

_____

_____

SUMMING UP CHAPTER 5

- We are made differently from one another, and we feel and function best when we live according to our own nature.

- According to ayurveda, there are three different energies that combine in varying degrees to make up your mind-body constitution. That remains with you throughout your life, but temporary imbalances in those energies throw you off so that you no longer feel like yourself. At first, that causes discomfort, but if it is allowed to go on, it can cause illness.

- By understanding your mind-body type and noticing early signs of imbalance, you can use diet and lifestyle to restore balance and prevent disease.

- Maintaining balance is a never-ending dance. You can't be perfect, but you can start by making healthy diet and lifestyle choices at least 51 percent of the time!

Part 3

The Mind Pathways

Chapter 6

Settling:

Take the Mindful Path to a Calm Mind

We can teach our minds to be calm and balanced; within this calmness is a richness and a potential, an inner knowledge which can render our lives boundlessly satisfying and meaningful. While the mind may be what traps us in unhealthy patterns of stress and imbalance, it is also the mind which can free us.

Tarthang Tulku

In the rush of daily life, in the noise of the world around and the monologue inside, the spacious clarity and energy of the natural mind are often lost to us. Settling the mind, being grounded in the present, allows you to work more skillfully with the thoughts, emotions, and experiences of life.

"My mind is so chaotic I can't even hear myself think," Alexandra said when we first met. She was a successful corporate executive with a high-pressure job, a twenty-year marriage, and two children. Several years before we met, she had lost her job in a corporate takeover and had been unemployed for over a year. Though she eventually landed a new job, she had, in the meantime, fallen into a major depressive episode of the anxious type. Antidepressant and antianxiety medications had been helpful for a brief period of time, but the side effects were now creating more distress than relief. Her best default strategy was to work harder, run ultra-marathons, and overcommit in her personal life. In that way she silenced her ruminating mind, at least during her daytime hours. Sleep eluded her, because whenever she slowed down and began to get in touch with thoughts or feelings, she felt overwhelmed and out of control. As she drove herself to exhaustion, the depression only intensified, and was now threatening her work and even her marriage. Her strategies just were not working.

We encouraged Alexandra to begin her inward journey with an effort to settle her mind. We introduced her to the concept of "monkey mind," an ancient Buddhist metaphor likening the unsettled mind to a troop of monkeys, shrieking and swinging wildly from branch to branch, always on the move. Unable to settle her mind's chaotic workings, Alexandra could not see clearly just how her strategies for coping with life were creating much of her suffering, feeding depression, and draining her resilience.

Just a Minute Meditation

Early in our work with Alexandra, we introduced the idea of the Just a Minute Meditation. This first step toward quieting the mind is simple, yet brings remarkable results. Here's how it is done, and we invite you to do it right now.

- Quiet your body and get comfortable, relaxing your body as much as you can. Close your eyes, if you wish, or simply soften your gaze and focus on the floor in front of you. This is a minute to completely rest.

- Take this minute to simply breathe naturally, at whatever pace and depth your breath is moving at the moment. Place your attention consciously on each breath, following it from beginning to end of the cycle of inhaling and exhaling. Allow your breathing to pause a bit at the end of the exhalation, and allow your breath to begin the inhalation on its own. You might choose to count the breaths to help focus your attention.

- If your mind wanders, simply bring it back to counting your breaths or sensing the movement of the breath in your body.

Reflection

Take some time to reflect on this simple experience by answering these questions.

- What physical sensations were you most aware of? Where in your body did you most feel your breath?

- How would you describe the qualities of your breath—the pace, depth, rhythm? Was it relaxed, constricted, rushed?

- What did you notice about your thoughts? Was your mind busy, quiet, agitated, still? How was it to catch your mind thinking and return to the breath?

There is no right answer to any of these questions, of course. The whole point is simply to pause and to shift focus from the thinking mind to the breathing body. When you focus on the breath, your central nervous system automatically quiets down, your mind begins to settle, and the body relaxes. This activates your natural healing potential.

THE PSYCHOLOGY OF MINDFULNESS

As Alexandra's mind began to quiet down, we introduced her to the *psychology of mindfulness*, a term we use to describe our approach to healing and transformation of suffering, which is based in Buddhist psychology and mindfulness practices.

Suffering and the Unsettled Mind

In Buddhist teachings, the analogy of the "first and second arrows" is used to explain the role of the unsettled mind in the creation of suffering. The first arrows of life strike us all in the form of the inevitable experiences of being human: illness, aging, loss of those we love, natural disasters, and the list goes on. The pain of these first arrows cannot be avoided. The second arrows, however, are within our control. The second arrows are those the mind creates in reaction to these painful experiences.

When we observe the mind carefully, we see how our thoughts and stories about the events of our lives add layers of unnecessary suffering to the original pain. The unsettled mind instinctively rejects and seeks to escape what is painful by grasping for diversion in what is pleasant or by emotionally shutting down and disconnecting altogether. Doing this, we cut ourselves off from the present moment's experience and engage in a futile attempt to change the reality of our experience, which only compounds our distress. These reactive and eventually habitual patterns of thoughts and feelings are the "second arrows," which are 100 percent self-inflicted.

In Alexandra's case, the second arrows began with her reaction to losing her job: harsh self-criticism, isolating herself from colleagues and friends because of the shame she felt, and frenetic activity that distracted her attention. She developed multiple fear-based disaster scenarios about her future, which increased her anxiety until she was paralyzed and unable to act in her own best interest. Her strategies of avoidance and frantic activity kept her from clearly seeing her situation and taking more constructive action.

Although it may seem paradoxical, the way out of the suffering caused by the second arrows is to give up the struggle to escape from what's painful, and to train the mind to remain with whatever is arising, nonjudgmentally and openly. This is the essence of the practice of mindfulness, which is at the core of our approach to healing. We cannot change the events that create our distress, but we can change our way of relating to the experience. Rather than being caught up in strategies of the thinking mind, we can learn to simply be present to the fullness of each moment without judgment and with friendly curiosity. This radical acceptance of what *is* can open the door to freedom from suffering.

If you have experienced depression, this sort of nonjudging acceptance may be difficult to imagine. You may have lived the reality that the mind can become your enemy, and may feel you have lost a few battles. The biochemistry of depression compounds the ordinary distress caused by the unsettled mind, leaving you feeling powerless over the negative rumination and anxiety. The second arrows you've been hit with may include the belief that you are defective or inadequate, or that if you just did it right this time, just tried harder or found the right doctor, program, therapist, or medication, your problems would be over. You may have a heavy dose of shame and the sense that you need to be fixed or to fix yourself. As a result of all of these mistaken beliefs, you may suffer from the illusion that you are separate and alone, that you don't belong to the rest of the human community.

What we want you to hear is that there is relief from your suffering. Through settling your mind and discovering the spacious awareness that is its nature, you can learn to relate even to painful experiences in a new way. You can move from struggle, avoidance, or disconnection to being more fully alive and aware in the moment, which is the only moment in which change occurs or joy can be found. The good medicine of mindfulness practice is the foundation of this transformation, and in the remaining chapters of this workbook, we will unfold the key elements of mindfulness practice as a pathway of healing and cultivating resilience.

THE GOOD MEDICINE OF MINDFULNESS

"I don't see what the benefit of all this mindfulness is," said Charles as he entered the room. "I've been excruciatingly mindful of how bad I'm feeling all week. It only makes things worse."

Charles suffers from the misconception that mindfulness is simply intensely feeling his emotions or paying particular attention to his thoughts. But mindfulness is more than that. Mindfulness is a particular *way* of noticing our experience—an intentional and curious way of looking at what's happening in any given moment, without having to label it good or bad, acceptable or not acceptable. Mindfulness is opening to the present moment, just as it is.

Mindfulness is more than an idea—it is a way of being. Living mindfully, we greet each experience with acceptance and give it our full attention. The unsettled mind, however, needs practice to develop this way of living. The remainder of this chapter offers tried-and-true practices that will help you begin to live more mindfully. We will start with activities that are already part of your everyday life. When you do them with intention and awareness, you will be able to capture the magic of the present moment—and your mind will settle of its own accord.

Mindfulness in Daily Life

Each moment of your daily routine offers you a chance to become more mindful, to calm your mind and live more fully in the present moment. Here are a few simple ways to begin:

- As you wake each morning, and before you get out of bed, do the Just a Minute Meditation (earlier in this chapter).

- Eat your breakfast mindfully, without reading the newspaper, watching television, or otherwise distracting yourself.

- When driving your car, turn off the radio. Pay attention to your hands on the steering wheel and consciously relax your grip.

- At a red light, focus on taking several full breaths.

- Use the ordinary sounds of daily life as a reminder to stop and breathe: the sound of the phone, the signal of arriving e-mail, and so forth. Or set your computer or other device to signal you at regular intervals to take a breathing break.

- Consider that housekeeping chores—like washing dishes or folding laundry—can be a time to tune in to your senses and be truly aware of what you're doing. If your mind wanders into planning or analyzing, simply return to the task at hand, concentrating on what you see, feel, smell, or hear.

- When walking from place to place, focus on the sensations in the body, like your feet touching the ground, the breeze on your face. Again, when the mind wanders, return to the body.

- As you prepare for bed, choose one activity to do mindfully, such as brushing your teeth or drinking a cup of herbal tea. Enjoy the sensations.

- As you drift off to sleep, practice conscious, mindful breathing.

MINDFUL EATING

The experience of eating a meal can be a rich exercise in fully appreciating the present moment. It provides several opportunities each day to strengthen your mindfulness skills.

Mindful Eating Instructions

Set aside a mealtime to eat alone or in silence with willing others.

- Put some thought beforehand into what you want to eat. Since you will pay greater attention to the food, you may wish to choose healthier, more wholesome and flavorful fare.

- Prepare the food with awareness and attention.

- Sit down, close your eyes, and allow the mind to quiet for a few moments. Give thanks for your food if you'd like.

- Before you take your first bite, notice the feeling of hunger in the belly, the sense of anticipation, the changes occurring in the mouth as it prepares to receive the food.

- Pay special attention to that first bite, how vividly you taste it, how the tongue and entire mouth come alive. Engage all of the senses: Look at the food, the shape and color and amount of it. Smell it before putting it in your mouth. Feel the warmth, substance, and texture as you touch it to your lips and then place it in your mouth. Taste each bite, noticing how different the experience of taste is in different areas of the mouth. You can even listen attentively to the sounds of the body enjoying a good meal.

- Chew each bite very slowly, resisting the urge to quickly swallow and move on to the next bite. Make each bite a deliberate act, one to be savored and enjoyed.

- Pay attention to the mechanics of eating, the movement of jaw and tongue, the way your body knows how to handle the food, chewing and moving it back toward the throat. Resist the urge to swallow until the food has been thoroughly chewed and the taste fully extracted. Then pay close attention to the act of swallowing.

- Continue in this way, returning to awareness of eating whenever the mind takes you somewhere else.

- Keep some of your awareness on your belly, noticing especially when you are beginning to feel satisfied, as though you have had enough. See if this happens and if you can stop eating *before* you have the sensation of fullness.

- Try to do this for at least part of each meal, and do it for an entire meal as often as you can.

WALKING MEDITATION

Walking meditation is a simple practice, and accessible even if you're one of those people who has difficulty sitting still! Walking meditation cultivates mindfulness but is also energizing and relaxing. You may walk inside in privacy, or choose to be out in the natural world. You might do this for an extended period of time—twenty or thirty minutes—or you might adapt it to any shorter period of walking you do during the day, such as walking to the water cooler or walking from your home to your car.

Walking Meditation Instructions

- Pay attention to your posture, being alert yet relaxed. Arms should be comfortably at your side.

- Your gaze should be soft and directed at the ground a couple of feet ahead of you. If you are walking outside, you may need to remain aware of your surroundings, but keep your gaze soft and receptive, without scanning or focusing on what surrounds you.

- Plant your feet firmly on the ground and place your attention on the sensations in your feet as they meet the ground. You might find it helpful to mentally note each step as a sequence of lifting, moving, and placing the foot.

- Be conscious of your breath, using it as another anchor for your attention. Let your breath be natural, and you might find that after a time, it becomes synchronized with your footsteps.

- You may vary your pace. If you are walking indoors, take smaller steps and move at a slower pace. If you are out of doors, walk at a pace that feels relaxed and easy.

- Enjoy your walking. There's no need to hurry, no pressure to arrive.

GOING DEEPER: MINDFULNESS MEDITATION PRACTICE

There are many misconceptions about meditation, some of which you might have heard. Mindfulness meditation is not stopping all thought. It is not a time to reflect on your current situation and come up with creative ideas. And it is not an effort to attain some rarefied state of bliss or escape from emotion. Meditation, as we practice and teach it, is the intentional activity of setting aside time to silently observe your own inner experience as it is in the moment. The daily living mindfulness practices described previously will help you to quiet your body and mind, but it's only in meditation that you literally train your attention to stay focused in the present moment, and eventually enter the state of spacious awareness and stillness that is at the center of monkey mind. The ability to settle the mind in this way is the starting point for the rest of the skills we teach in the following chapters of this book.

In order to develop some consistency, we suggest that you find a regular time of day to set aside for meditation; when you do so, meditation becomes a habit, like the habit of eating breakfast. Busy schedules, interruptions, lack of support from others, and your own discomfort with silence are all challenges to developing a meditation practice. We wholeheartedly suggest that, if at all possible, you find a teacher and others to meditate with, and, if that's not possible, that you find a reliable source of information and guided meditations.

For more resources, including a recorded version of the instructions that follow, visit our website: www.partnersinresilience.com.

Instructions for Seated Meditation

- Sit comfortably on a meditation cushion, bench, or chair. Your back should be upright but not rigid, and your shoulders open but relaxed. Your head should be aligned with your spine, chin slightly lowered.

- You may close your eyes or allow them to remain slightly open and fixed at a point on the floor two to three feet ahead of you.

- Place the tip of your tongue on your palate just behind and above your teeth, and soften your face and relax the jaw, breathing through your nose.

- Check your position and see if you need to shift it to be more comfortable or more upright and alert. It is fine to shift your body later, if discomfort interferes with your meditation. Simply move slowly and mindfully to rearrange your posture.

- Once you have settled into a comfortable position, shift your awareness to your breath. Follow the breath for a few complete cycles, noting the movement in the belly or the sensation of air entering and leaving your nostrils.

- Using your breath as anchor, simply sit in silence. When you realize that your mind has wandered into thought, just notice that and, without judgment, return your attention to your breath. This is the practice of mindfulness, so there is no need to strive for anything else. Returning—again and again—to the present moment *is* the practice.

- From time to time, your attention may also expand to include body sensations. Those, too, can be the objects of your awareness. Practice noting these sensations without labeling them as pleasant or unpleasant, but simply experiencing them in the body.

- The same will be true for sound or movement in the space around you. Rather than being a distraction, these occurrences can become another focus of your awareness in the present moment. Again, practice experiencing them without labeling them in the mind. Simply notice.

- Of course, thought will arise, and sometimes you'll find yourself far down the path into a story you're telling yourself or a plan you're developing. This is what the mind does, so it is no problem. When you notice this has happened, simply return to your anchor in the breath. The practice of mindfulness meditation helps develop what is called the "observing self": a part of you that can see what's happening while you are experiencing it. It is as if you're seated on the banks of a river, watching the stream of thought and feeling. One after another, thoughts flow into view and away. There's no need to follow them; you can simply sit.

- When you do notice that you have become distracted and your awareness has weakened, use that as a moment of mindfulness. This is the practice of training the mind to stay present, and eventually it will naturally settle.

- In every moment of mindfulness, remember that this is a practice grounded in gentleness, with no good or bad, right or wrong. This is not a self-improvement project or a competition.

THE BENEFITS OF MINDFULNESS MEDITATION PRACTICE

The practice of mindfulness is transformational. Those who practice consistently report:

- A greater sense of well-being

- The development of an "observing self" that gives a larger perspective on thoughts and emotions

- Insight into patterns of thought and behavior, and the freedom to choose options other than habitual, reactive patterns

- The ability to stay with experience, to recognize its impermanence and have hope for the future

- Healing of disconnection from self (body, heart, and mind)

- Fuller acceptance of life as it is—suffering and all

- Greater capacity for joy, as a result of living in the present moment rather than the past or the future

The net gain of this transformation was simply and joyfully expressed by Alexandra when she said, "Now I can see just how my twisted thinking and my running away from myself brought me so much more suffering than I needed to have. And now, having allowed myself to be present with it all, I still feel the pain of losing my job, but every day, I feel joy, too." This awareness of the possibility of joy even in the midst of life's painful experiences is at the heart of mindful living. The Taoist expression captures it all: life is "ten thousand joys and ten thousand sorrows."

Neuroscience and Meditation

Modern science, aided by the development of technology, has revealed the astonishing truth that mindfulness meditation practice changes the structure and function of the brain.

In general, meditators appear to have a quieter limbic system, decreased density in the amygdala, and strong, robust prefrontal lobes. What this translates into is less emotional reactivity, increased emotional self-control, improved stress management, and moderation of the stress response.

This was demonstrated in a research project conducted by Eileen Luders (2009), a researcher in the Department of Neurology at UCLA. Using a high-resolution MRI, Luders and her colleagues compared the brains of twenty-two meditators and twenty-two age-matched nonmeditators and found that the meditators had more gray matter in regions of the brain that are important for attention, emotion regulation, and mental flexibility. Specifically, meditators showed significantly larger volumes in the area of the hippocampus, the orbitofrontal cortex, the thalamus, and the inferior temporal gyrus—all of which are known for regulating emotions. Because these areas of the brain are closely linked to emotion, Luders notes that they might be the neuronal basis of meditators' outstanding ability to regulate their emotions and respond to the ups and downs of everyday life.

A recent study by Massachusetts General Hospital and Harvard University put twenty-six highly stressed adults through an eight-week mindfulness-based stress reduction course. Brain scans were taken before and after the intervention, along with participants' own reports of stress. The participants who reported decreased stress also showed decreases in gray matter density in the amygdala. Previous research had revealed that trauma and chronic stress can enlarge the amygdala and make it more reactive and more connected to other areas of the brain, leading to greater stress and anxiety. This study is one of the first documented cases showing change occurring in the opposite direction—with the brain instead becoming less reactive and more resilient (Kilpatrick et al. 2011).

SUMMING UP CHAPTER 6

- The resilient mind is a calm and grounded mind.

- While we cannot escape the suffering of this human life—including depression and anxiety—we can learn to minimize the additional suffering that is created by our own minds.

- Through the practice of mindfulness in its various forms we can quiet the mind. In the spaciousness of the settled mind we can open to the full range of our life experience with equanimity.

- Scientific research now confirms that mindfulness meditation is a means of quieting the stress response, improving emotional regulation, and improving our sense of well-being.

Chapter 7

Opening:

Develop Emotional Resilience

Let everything happen to you,
Beauty and terror.
Just keep going.
No feeling is final.

Rainer Maria Rilke

Imagine a life without emotions: No joy at the birth of a new baby. No grief at the loss of a loved one. No compassion at the plight of tsunami victims. No love providing the glue in relationships. No fear to warn of danger or anger to motivate the fight for justice. No small morning delights like the sight of a cardinal outside the window or that first cup of coffee on the porch.

Emotions are the key to understanding who you are: what you are attracted to or repelled by, what motivates you, and what threatens your safety. Emotions can operate as a navigational device—an inner GPS of sorts—letting you know where you are, suggesting where you might wish to go, guiding you on your way. They are a source of pleasure in daily life and a source of the empathy that enables you to connect with others. By learning to read your inner emotional language—becoming emotionally literate—you can understand yourself more completely, navigate through your daily challenges more skillfully, and appreciate the richness of life more fully.

However, emotional life has its complications and difficulties. You may have developed rules and beliefs that distort your view of emotions and your ways of expressing them. You may have learned to distrust emotions or see them as a sign of weakness. Perhaps you keep them to yourself, having found that others are not able or willing to hear about them. You might even have shut down the most painful emotions to protect yourself from feeling distress. Unfortunately, disconnection from emotions may leave your inner life feeling empty or unknown to you.

If depression clouds the picture, emotions can become a fearful place to enter—a dangerous neighborhood on a dark night. If you've been consumed by sadness, guilt, or hopelessness, the hallmarks of depression, you may have become emotionally phobic: afraid to experience certain emotions lest you find yourself caught again in the grip of depression.

In this chapter you will find tools to enable you to move freely in your inner world of emotional experience, however constrained it might now be as a result of your life experiences. This freedom to feel everything fully is one of the foundational skills for recovering and maintaining your resilience, preventing recurrence of depression, and living a joyful life.

UNDERSTANDING THE FLOW OF EMOTIONAL EXPERIENCE

Emotions function naturally as the moment-to-moment response to the happenings of your everyday life. They might be likened to weather fronts: arriving, remaining for a time, and moving on. Emotions originate in the limbic system—the "emotional brain"—and as the limbic brain responds to stimuli around you, neurotransmitters linked to various emotional states are released. These chemicals travel along neural pathways to the frontal lobes of your cortex—the "thinking brain"—where you add thoughts and memories to the mix. These thoughts and memories of previous experience enable you to describe, interpret, communicate, and decide how to act on your emotions. It is at this point that emotional life can get complicated.

In the last chapter we introduced the idea of "monkey mind": the untrained, unsettled mind that is so often the source of suffering. When you are captive in monkey mind, you are vulnerable to believing that your thoughts are reality, and can become caught in a web of storytelling that can lead you into a deep morass of painful feelings. These "second arrows" of thought can add layers of misery to the original emotional experience, which might have been difficult enough as it was.

Consider this everyday example.

• Kathryn's Story

Kathryn is sitting at her desk when an e-mail from her younger brother appears. The news isn't good; her father's cancer has returned, and the biopsy says it's the aggressive type. Her first reaction is instinctual: shock and fear are felt as tightness in her chest, shakiness, and a cold, sinking sensation in her belly. Then her thinking mind adds words to the physical sensations: This is impossible! He seems so well, so strong for his age. How can this be? *She imagines the worst possible scenarios:* This time there will be no possible treatment. He will suffer a painful death, and the grief and needs of my mother will be consuming.

Kathryn has moved into the realm of the second arrows. She is no longer in the present, but in the unknown future, telling herself a story created by her anxious mind. She begins to feel overwhelmed, despairing, and unable to handle her feelings. She chastises herself for being so weak, so frightened. Unable to concentrate on work, she spends the rest of the day preoccupied with her inner thoughts and feelings. She turns off her cell phone to avoid any more conversations with the family. When her children come home from school, they find her distant and withdrawn, unlike her usual self. Bewildered, they leave the house to find a friendly neighbor.

• John's Story

Her brother John has reacted to the same situation in a very different way. Although the news is disturbing, he bypasses the body sensations and moves directly into thinking mode. He clicks into action, alerting the rest of the family and contacting an oncologist friend to assess the prognosis. He believes that action is the best response, recalling his father's mantra: "There's nothing to be afraid of. Just get moving." *Determined not to feel, he notices a bit of sadness while talking with his wife but quickly moves away from it, distracting himself with video games until the early hours of the morning.*

John had experienced a major depressive episode years ago, and any sign of sadness is now a warning for him. He chooses to distract himself and remain comfortably numb, rather than feel the sadness he fears may send him into the sinkhole of depression. His wife feels worried about him but is shut out and unable to approach him. She goes to bed, alone with her feelings, wondering if they will ever connect around their fears or sadness.

The Emotional Response Continuum

One way to look at John's and Kathryn's responses (and yours as well) is to see them along a continuum. This continuum of emotional experience ranges from disconnected (unaware of emotions) to flooded (overwhelmed by them).

Disconnected	Resistant	Open	Fixated	Flooded
No awareness of emotion in the body or mind	Aware of emotion but turning away to avoid feeling	Able to sense and fully experience the emotion	Intensely feeling and having difficulty moving away from the emotion	Overwhelmed or paralyzed by emotion

DISCONNECTED

When you are *disconnected* from emotional experience, there is no awareness of emotion in your body or thoughts. This is an extreme pattern, though it may be true of anyone from time to time. When you are disconnected from your experience of emotion, you are living at a distance from your life experience, and might feel empty or distant from yourself and others.

RESISTANT

In the examples above, John illustrates the *resistant* mode of response. When you resist your feelings, there is a conscious (or sometimes automatic) decision to turn away from them, to avoid feeling their pain. Resisting is based on fears that something bad will happen or you won't be able to deal with the emotion. This may result in other distressing feelings, like tension or irritation. It takes energy to sustain resistance, and you miss the possibility to realize the wisdom of your emotions. While it's natural to slip into this mode at times of great distress, resisting becomes problematic when it is your regular mode of dealing with emotions. If you are mindful and recognize the pattern as a problem, you can learn to shift your response toward the *open* mode.

FIXATED

To *fixate*—to become obsessed or preoccupied—is another common but problematic response and the one that Kathryn experienced. In this pattern, your felt emotion becomes complicated by your thinking mind. The thoughts and stories it generates only prolong and intensify the distress. The natural cycle of emotion—to arrive, stay for a time, and pass—is blocked, and it's difficult to let the emotion pass. You become preoccupied and unable to engage with the things that need your attention. Unable to find your center, your *observing self*, you're caught in a torrent of feelings and can't determine a course of action or care for yourself. Again, this pattern can happen from time to time, but becomes problematic when it occurs regularly. Maintaining mindfulness is the key to shifting out of fixation to the more fluid *open* response.

FLOODED

In this extreme state you might find yourself totally incapacitated by emotion and possibly acting in ways that are damaging to yourself or to others. While this is less common, being overwhelmed emotionally this way may contribute to shame and self-criticism, triggers of depression. The following chapter will provide more detail and tools for coping with flooding.

OPEN

Remaining open, turning toward and embracing all of your feelings, is the key to emotional resilience. When you are able to open with mindfulness, paying attention to sensations in the body, noticing thoughts and their effects without being carried away into the past or the future, the emotion goes through its natural life cycle. Being present through this full cycle can enrich your life and open doors to understanding yourself and your situation. In the remainder of this chapter we'll be giving you information and tools to help you develop this important capacity.

Assessing Your Emotional Response Patterns

One step on the path to emotional resilience is identifying your own patterns of experiencing emotions as they arise: your own tendencies to move to various positions on the emotional response continuum. Like everyone, you have developed your own "emotional comfort zone" that includes feelings that you welcome or seek out, while there are more painful or difficult emotions that you avoid or feel flooded by.

To increase awareness of your own emotional response patterns, sort the following list of emotions into the three categories in the table that follows it.

Worry	Happiness	Excitement	Joy
Helplessness	Embarrassment	Anger	Despair
Confusion	Loneliness	Fear	Discouragement
Shame	Jealousy	Frustration	Confidence
Rage	Grief	Hurt	Hopelessness
Anxiety	Contentment	Terror	Passion
Irritation	Calm	Pride	Gratitude
Pleasure	Love	Sadness	Restlessness

Emotions I resist, avoid, or am disconnected from	Emotions I am open to and comfortable feeling completely	Emotions I find overwhelming or get fixated on

To make the best use of this information, reflect on your categories and answer these questions:

- Which emotions do I regularly resist or disconnect from? Why might that be the case? (What are the beliefs, rules, or actions of mine that underlie this pattern?)

- Of these emotions, which of them might I begin to open to?

- Which emotions do I often become fixated on or feel flooded by? Why might that be the case? (What are the beliefs, fears, or actions of mine that underlie this pattern?)

- Which of *these* emotions might I begin to open to?

- What emotions am I open to and comfortable with?

DEVELOPING EMOTIONAL FLOW

The good news is that any problematic response patterns you may have learned can be unlearned, and you can move toward a more open mode of responding to your daily flow of feelings. The tools in the next sections of this chapter—along with your practice of mindfulness meditation as taught in the preceding chapter—are just what you need for beginning the change process.

Although this might seem to be a daunting task, we encourage you to look at the benefits. Opening to *all* of your emotions enables you to:

- Attend to situations that need a response rather than ignore them until they get worse.

- Tap into your creative energy rather than shutting it down along with your emotions.

- Become more vitally alive, even in your darker moments.

Being open to your full range of emotions is also critical in recovering from and preventing depression. As you become more skillful in dealing with the difficult emotions, you will gain confidence that they do not always lead to another depressive episode. As you begin to trust yourself and your emotions, you will be able to distinguish normal "blue moods" from those that might really tip you into depression. Then you can take action early enough to prevent that from happening.

Living in the Open Mode

Shifting back to look at Kathryn's and John's stories, let's imagine what their experiences might look like had they been mindfully open to their emotions rather than being fixated or resisting.

• Kathryn's and John's Stories Revisited

Upon hearing his father's news, John notices sensations of shock and fear coursing through his body. He tells himself that it is normal and he can handle it. He names these feelings and takes a few deep breaths to get centered before he responds to his father with words of concern and his wish to be of help. He listens to his father's needs and, together with him, begins to develop a plan of action: he'll let the rest of his siblings know, and he'll call an oncologist friend to help them all understand the situation more clearly. He's able to ask questions and listen sensitively to his father, who expresses gratitude. John hangs up the phone, feeling close to his dad and happy to be of help. He realizes that he's not only fearful, but also sad that his father, who's already had a difficult life, will have to suffer more. He's aware that he, too, is vulnerable and should have his PSA checked at his next physical exam. A bit of anxiety about his own mortality pops up, and he notices this but refocuses on the present moment. He thinks about sending an e-mail to his sister Kathryn, but picks up the phone instead because he wants to share his feelings with her and knows it will be comforting to them both to share this moment.

He's right about that. Kathryn picks up the phone and feels the same body sensations of shock and fear when she hears the news. Tears come to her eyes, and her throat tightens. She notes all of these feelings and, with a few deep breaths, reminds herself to just be present, to listen to John, to let her thinking mind come into play so she can understand exactly what's happening. Kathryn is able to let John know how she is feeling, and to ask how he is. As they share this moment, both Kathryn and John feel connected and supported by each other, grateful that they can share this together. Feeling some-what relieved, though still anxious and sad, they both move into their days. Kathryn talks with her parents about the news and then rearranges some of her work deadlines so she can spend a day or two with them. She makes a cup of tea and sits quietly, allowing all of her feelings to simply come up in her awareness, stay for a while, and—as she comforts herself—pass away. Her emotions leave some traces that she knows will be with her the rest of the day, but they are manageable. When her children arrive home, she's able to be present with them, listening to their news and feeling the joy and comfort that their youthful energy and excitement bring to her.

John calls his wife and briefly shares the news, and they plan to have dinner together at one of their favorite restaurants. Over the meal, he shares the details of the news and his own feelings about it. She feels included and connected, and is able to share her feelings as well. Both of them feel the presence of sadness and fear as they talk. John shares his concern about depression creeping back in, and she's able to assure him that she'll be watching and supporting him. They leave for home, feeling deeply grateful for their love for each other and their family roots. Later that evening they share the day's experiences with neighbors while watching happy children run through the sprinklers. They see goodness all around them and feel joy, even on a day like this.

John and Kathryn, in the second scenario, had learned to mindfully attend to their emotions and were not caught in tendencies to disconnect, resist, fixate, or be flooded by them. They were able to stay open to their emotions as they arose, name them, and experience them fully, allowing them to run their natural course. By turning skillfully toward their feelings, however painful, they could also experience the warm reassurance of connection and the joy of the day. They felt capable of moving into the future, regardless of what it might bring.

EXPERIENCING THE FULL CYCLE OF EMOTION

This sort of emotional resilience begins by mindfully opening to your emotional experience and flowing with the natural emotional ups and downs of your daily life. As you develop mindfulness of the full cycle of feelings, even the very painful ones will be easier to tolerate. In fact, you will find that fully experiencing the cycle of an emotion with mindfulness—nonjudging and friendly acceptance—may be a relief, a type of catharsis.

The idea of fully experiencing painful feelings might be frightening to you if you are in the middle of an episode of severe depression, and it's best to wait until the intensity of such an episode has lifted. Still, it is safe to open yourself to the natural flow of minor daily emotional ups and downs. As your emotional comfort zone expands, you will gain confidence for the stronger emotions to come, and become more present and engaged in your life.

For the following meditation, select an emotion from the emotional response pattern exercise that you often avoid or that you find somewhat overwhelming. Don't choose the most extreme or overwhelming emotion—just a normal, everyday emotion. Choose one that has some charge for you but is not too strong.

Guided Meditation: Sensing Emotion in the Body

- Sit comfortably, in a chair or on cushions, and align your body in a position that is alert but relaxed.

- Ground yourself for a few minutes by paying conscious attention to the full cycle of your breath, noticing the rise and fall of your belly or the air entering and leaving your nostrils. If, at any point in the meditation, you find yourself feeling overwhelmed by the emotional sensations that come up, you can return to simple awareness of the breath as an anchor.

Remember to use the spirit of mindful, nonjudging curiosity as you explore your experience.

- When you feel ready, call to mind the emotion you have chosen to work with. It may be a feeling of frustration or anger, a sadness, a fear. Allow your memory to recall the details of the situation in which this emotion appeared: the place, people, words, or actions that were the triggers for this feeling.

- As you recall these details, try to get in touch with the physical sensations in your body. Emotions are most often felt in the body between your throat and your groin. Where are you feeling it now?

- Notice the quality of the sensation? Is it hot, cold, tight, tingly? Is it mild or intense?

- Is the sensation moving, or is it settling in some part of your body?

- If thoughts or stories about the emotion enter your mind, simply notice that, and notice the effect of the thoughts on the sensations you are feeling in your body. You might notice that the quality and intensity of the sensations wax and wane as thought appears. Notice that the emotional experience is like a wave, expanding and contracting. See if you can simply ride the wave, dropping thought and story line and simply sitting with the sensation as it rises and falls.

- You might also notice that the emotion itself will change over the course of time. Perhaps you began with anger, and it dissolves into fear or grief. It is the nature of the emotional life to be complex and sometimes multilayered. All of it is important to explore.

- Give yourself as completely as you can to the flow of the emotion and its changes. You may notice that it builds, reaches a peak, and then begins to subside. If you've experienced the full cycle of the emotion, notice how you feel after the wave of feeling has subsided. If you have not had a complete experience of the emotion, know that you can return to this process and work through the feeling at your own pace, and you can also do this in your everyday life experience.

- End this meditation with a few cycles of simple awareness of your breath, allowing whatever emotional sensation remains in your body to pass. It may help to send a gentle instruction to yourself to let go of these emotions for now. Take time to allow this to happen, and for your body and mind to return to as quiet a state as is possible right now. Appreciate your experience for whatever awareness it has brought to you.

Reflecting on This Meditation

Writing your reflections on this meditation can anchor your felt experience in your thinking mind. This may help you to transfer the learning to your daily life experience, which is the ultimate goal of this exercise.

Answer the following questions, and also note any other questions or observations that come to you as you reflect.

What emotions did I experience? Did they change during the course of the meditation? How?

_____

_____

Where in the body did I sense each of the emotions I experienced? How would I describe these sensations? How did they change over the course of the meditation?

_____

_____

Were my emotions easy to recognize and name, or did I have trouble identifying what they were? How familiar were they?

_____

_____

What thoughts did I have during this experience? How did they affect the emotions I was feeling?

_____

_____

What was it like to be with these emotions without distracting myself or otherwise shutting down?

_____

_____

How was it for me to let the emotion pass?

_____

_____

In summary, what did I learn about my way of being with these difficult emotions?

_____

_____

_____

MOVING DEEPER: WORKING WITH DIFFICULT EMOTIONS

As you worked through the meditation on sensing emotion in the body, you might have wondered, as many do, just what to do when your emotions seem to demand some sort of response or action. After all, these emotions can be complex and they occur in the context of real life. Often they present you with a problem to be solved, or they leave you with a level of distress that doesn't seem to pass on its own. The following six-step process will provide you with a way to work through your difficult life experiences, using emotions as a guide to your inner wisdom.

Step one: Simply notice. Begin with awareness of the emotion in your body and mind. Ask, *What is happening now?* This will include body sensations, thoughts, and perhaps memories.

Step two: Invite and open. It might seem more natural to distract yourself from difficult feelings, but with mindful curiosity you can say yes to everything that is coming up. It's helpful to silently say to yourself *yes,* or *just open,* in order to counteract the natural tendency to contract with resistance. Remember the spirit of mindfulness, which is nonjudging acceptance of whatever is appearing at the moment. Simply notice all your reactions, even the resistance, and open to them. Consciously relax your body and remember to breathe mindfully.

Step three: Explore the causes. At this point it is helpful to ask *Why am I feeling this? What words, interactions, or other factors came together with my own sensitivities to create this response?* This is not done in the spirit of blaming someone or something for our responses, but in the search for understanding in order to respond skillfully.

Step four: Identify possible actions. Sometimes, listening to your emotional responses and understanding their causes will suggest a course of action to be taken in the moment. For example, if anger has been triggered by hurtful words from your friend, an appropriate response would be to find a way to express yourself to that friend. At other times the action may need to wait until a later time. For example, if it is too hard to express yourself to your friend, you might seek help to develop your own assertiveness so that the next time, you can respond immediately. If you see actions that can be taken in the moment, take them. If they must be postponed, just mentally note those actions and move on to the next step in this process.

Step five: Care for yourself. Whether or not there are constructive actions to take, you can always be aware of whether these emotions have left you in need of some attention. You might wish to seek out the support of a friendly listener you trust. But often the person most able to give you exactly what you need is *you*. Perhaps it's comfort, some expression such as "Yes, I know, this is really painful." Or you might need to hear some sort of affirmation like "This is difficult, but you did a good job of handling it." You might need some basic self-care such as sleep, exercise, or a comforting cup of tea. Listening carefully, you can befriend yourself.

Step six: Allow the feelings to pass. When all is said and done, feelings sometimes linger. Some feelings are simply more intense than others, and some situations need to be reworked multiple times. However, it is important to know when you are simply holding on too tight, or reigniting the flames of the emotion by replaying the story in your mind. It's human to hold on, and it might take a conscious decision to be willing to let go. Some emotions have a long half-life, and while you are waiting for them to pass, it helps to simply accept and allow, releasing the stories you tell yourself about them.

Working Skillfully with Emotions

This exercise is designed to help you use this six-step process in a real-life situation of your own. You may choose the same experience as you did in the previous meditation or choose another.

First, sit quietly for a few minutes and recall the situation in as much detail as possible, noting the setting, the situation, or interactions that triggered the feelings, words that might have been spoken, and so forth. If you can, recall the emotions as they appeared, as they intensified, and how the experience ended, noting your body sensations, thoughts, and actions. Record your description below.

_____

_____

_____

_____

_____

_____

_____

_____

_____

_____

Next, using the grid below, you can analyze your experience, noting (without judgment!) what your experience was at each point in the process. In the last column, note your insights and ideas about handling such situations even more skillfully in the future. You'll find that the process as described previously will give you some ideas, and your own insights will also arise. Remember, there are no wrong answers.

Step	My Experience	Reflections and Insights
Step one: Simply notice.		
Step two: Invite and open.		
Step three: Explore the causes.		
Step four: Identify possible actions.		
Step five: Care for yourself.		
Step six: Allow the feelings to pass.		

LAST BUT NOT LEAST: OPEN TO WHAT IS PLEASANT

As you've worked through this chapter, you've gained insights and skills for working with the daily emotional experiences that are difficult, that cause distress. This is the most obvious, but not the only, pathway to becoming more emotionally resilient.

As a human being, you are hardwired to scan the environment for danger, for what seems potentially threatening. This is a good thing if you're surrounded by actual threats, but as a natural default it creates the tendency to pay attention to only half of what's happening. The other half is a rich storehouse of pleasure, renewal, and joy, all of which feed emotional resilience.

Henri Nouwen, a Catholic priest and author who suffered with depression himself, wrote, "Joy does not simply happen to us. We have to choose joy and keep choosing it every day" (Nouwen 1994, 29). This is a provocative statement. What does it mean to "choose joy"?

In terms of emotional resilience, choosing joy is choosing to open fully to those experiences we often overlook, those that are not so threatening that they grab our survival-minded attention. They can be the big events of life: births, weddings, holidays, new beginnings of all sorts. Or they can be small happenings: the laughter of playing children, the call of a loon at dusk on a summer evening, a warm look in the eyes of a good friend across the dinner table, celebrating your favorite baseball team's victory from the bleacher seats on a warm summer evening.

Paying deliberate attention to what is pleasant requires that we choose, over and over again, to take the time to open to what's happening in these moments. When did you last really watch the sun set—really open to the entire, amazing show of color rather than simply give it a quick glance? When was the last time you really felt your child's hug, as you looked deeply into his face? Or tasted the first ripe raspberry of summer? Your busy life and your attention to what's coming up next can keep you from settling deeply into the moments that bring joy.

Mindfulness in daily life is an antidote to these natural tendencies. Developing the habit of looking for what's pleasant, opening to it, and planting it firmly in your conscious awareness will pay great dividends. This simple "three pleasures" exercise takes only a few moments each day, and is one way to cultivate the habit of mindful attention to what you often miss seeing.

Three Pleasures Exercise

1. At the end of the day, give yourself some time for written reflection. You may wish to use a special notebook or journal for this practice.

2. After sitting quietly for a few minutes, reflect on and record three pleasures that came your way today. At first it might be difficult, but with practice it will become more natural. If you have trouble beginning, you might try recalling your day chronologically. Or you might use the simple structure of recalling pleasant things that came by way of your senses: sight,

sound, smell, taste, touch. Or scan through your interactions with people today, recalling kind words or favors or sharing of news.

3. As you write, take time to recall these events in detail, and open to the sensations in your body and thoughts that fill your mind. Let the pleasures sink in, and really enjoy them. Write them down in as much detail as you can.

4. In the morning anticipate any pleasant things the new day might bring, and set your intention to be open to surprises as well.

5. During the day take time to savor the pleasures of the day by recalling them in a quiet moment or sharing them with a friend. Telling the stories to another is a way of generating more pleasure and of anchoring the experience in your awareness.

SUMMING UP CHAPTER 7

- Emotional resilience is the capacity to open fully to the daily ups and downs of your emotional experience with mindful, nonjudging acceptance.

- Emotions are a fundamental human experience essential to your survival. Every emotional experience has a natural cycle of flow: it arrives, remains for a while, and passes. No emotion is permanent.

- Due to early learning or other experiences, you might have developed patterns of emotional experiencing that interrupt that flow; your emotional life might be limited by disconnection, resistance, fixation, or flooding.

- Working with these patterns using mindfulness skills and your own insight can undo them and allow you to open to all emotions in a way that makes you resilient and brings you fully alive.

- Opening fully to pleasant emotional experiences will balance your perspective and be a source of joy.

Chapter 8

Knowing:

Become a Source of Wisdom for Yourself

*There is a great deal of unmapped country within us, which would have
to be taken into account in an exploration of our gusts and storms.*

George Eliot

Lauren teared up as she slumped onto the couch in the therapy office. "I don't know what happened," she said. "One minute I was working on a paper for my freshman English class and thirty minutes later I was crying in my room. I felt just hopeless and I've been depressed ever since. But the worst thing is that I don't know why. I feel like I'm going crazy."

Lauren isn't going crazy but she *is* a stranger to herself. She must get to know her unmapped inner territory in order to understand what happens when she is overtaken by such strong emotion. She needs to understand herself more completely in order to work more skillfully with all that is happening within.

Most people can identify a time when they felt taken over by a sudden, intense feeling that sprang from nowhere, and many regret the impulsive acts that these feelings prompted. Besides being unpleasant or frightening, these emotional storms can sometimes open the door to an episode of depression, as Lauren feared was happening to her.

What happened to Lauren could be considered an emotional tsunami: the kind of emotionally overwhelming experience that can knock you off your feet. In this chapter we will guide you to take a closer look at a time when you were overtaken by such a storm. There are two reasons it is important to look more closely at these very unpleasant experiences. First, it is helpful to see that these are common human reactions and they do not mean that you are going crazy or are out of control. Second, as you learn more about your own unmapped territory, you will feel more confident about your ability to handle such emotionally overwhelming experiences and will have more courage when faced with them.

THE EMOTIONAL TSUNAMI

It is inevitable that you are unaware of parts of your inner world. Everyone is. You spend most of the day dealing with the outside world: making a living, relating to others, navigating the streets of daily life. Naturally you are more familiar with the parts of yourself that you need in order to manage everyday life. You may even be tempted to arrange your life so you can stay within your comfort zone. You may want to avoid experiences that disturb you and stay away from people who might upset you. You may especially want to avoid the things within yourself that worry or confuse you. As long as you feel in control of the outside and the inside world, you feel pretty safe. However, none of us can maintain that kind of control at all times. An illness, a loss, a rejection, a threatening thought—all of these experiences come with the territory of being human.

To a greater or lesser degree, emotional tsunamis happen to everyone, and when they arrive, they threaten your sense of predictability and control. The good news is that it is possible to learn from them and reduce the harm they can cause. With the assistance of mindful strategies, you can learn to recognize an emotional storm in its earliest stages, slow things down when the wind picks up, and stop yourself from acting in ways that add to the damage. It is even possible to learn enough from your storm experiences that you can avoid them in the future.

Working with the Emotional Tsunami

Recall a time when you had an overwhelming experience like Lauren's. Maybe you felt a sudden hollowing in your stomach and all of your energy seemed to drain away, or maybe someone seemed to ignore you and you were filled with anger. Perhaps in the middle of a gathering, you experienced a feeling of loneliness and felt hopeless about ever belonging anywhere. After you read the following description of Lauren's review of her experience, take some time to write about one of your own emotional tsunamis.

Lauren's Story

"I was sitting at the library, trying to write a review of Moby Dick. *I didn't like the book and I couldn't seem to get started. I was starting to worry about getting it done on time. I overheard some people at the table behind me. It was my roommate, Tiffany, and three other girls from my dorm. Earlier, I had asked Tiffany if she wanted to study with me, but she said no, she wanted to go work out. But then there she was in the library with those girls she's been hanging out with more and more. I got this sick feeling in my stomach, and suddenly I had to get out of the library. I ran into the deli on my way back to the dorm and bought a big bag of M&M's. By the time I got to my room, I had eaten half of it. I was starting to feel sicker. I was crying and kept eating the candy. I remember thinking that I was never going to make friends at college. I heard this voice in my head saying,* I told you so; I told you nobody likes you. *I've felt horrible ever since, and I ended up starting a fight with Tiffany the next day. We haven't talked to each since then and I don't know what to say to her."*

Your Experience:

_____

_____

_____

_____

_____

_____

_____

_____

_____

Now go back and reread Lauren's story, looking for lapses in her awareness. At the beginning she was aware of her thoughts about writing and her worry about finishing. But once she saw Tiffany with the others, she felt compelled to leave the library, to buy the candy, and to mindlessly eat it. What happened between those two moments? Lauren didn't lose her mind, as she'd feared, but she did lose her mindfulness. She couldn't come up with reasons for her behavior or for the strong anger that she felt toward

Tiffany. The box explains what can happen in the brain that makes mindfulness so hard to hold on to. You will see that Lauren's experience (and perhaps yours) sounds suspiciously like an *amygdala hijack*.

A Hurricane in the Brain

Daniel Goleman, author of *Emotional Intelligence: Why It Can Matter More Than IQ* (1995, 18), coined the term "amygdala hijack." Such a hijack occurs when the emotional system of the brain acts independently of the thinking part of the brain. Normally, information that the senses take in is sent to the thalamus. The thalamus usually relays that information to the neocortex (the reasoning part of the brain). From the neocortex it is then sent to the amygdala, the part of the emotional brain that sends out alarms to the rest of the body.

In this way, thinking and feeling are coordinated. But under conditions of threat, the thalamus bypasses the neocortex and the emotional brain reacts without any of the moderating influence that thinking can provide. According to Goleman, an amygdala hijack is characterized by three things:

- Strong emotional reaction

- Sudden onset

- Realizing after the fact that the reaction was inappropriate

---

Emotional tsunamis happen outside of your awareness, often leaving destruction in their wake. How might it turn out differently if you could bring mindful awareness right into the middle of such an intense, negative experience?

MAPPING THE PATH OF THE STORM

Using a combination of reflection, visualizing, and journaling, Lauren was able to describe her experience in much more detail. With guidance she was able to follow the path of the storm from sensation to thought to interpretation to action. She breathed a sigh of relief that it "made sense." She wasn't going crazy after all. The following description includes Lauren's closer examination of her experience, along with opportunities for bringing mindfulness into the heart of the storm.

The Rising of Sensation

Lauren remembered that when she had heard Tiffany's voice and seen the girls together, she had felt a tightening in her shoulders and a sensation of hollowness in her stomach. Had Lauren been able to notice these sensations and recognize them as the beginning of a negative reaction, she might have been able to use them as warning signs that a storm might be on the way. Instead, she had no awareness of them as they occurred.

FINDING THE POSSIBILITIES FOR MINDFULNESS

- Use the Just a Minute Meditation (see chapter 6) to slow things down.

- Recognize and name what is happening ("tight shoulders," "sinking feeling in stomach").

- Focus awareness on body sensations; it can take the punch out of the storm.

The Entry of Thought

Lauren identified the following series of thoughts: *There is Tiffany with Mary and Fiona. I had asked Tiffany to study with me and she said she wanted to work out. Now she's here with them.*

At this point, Lauren was objectively describing events to herself. There was no judging or evaluating going on; she was just noting what happened.

FINDING THE POSSIBILITIES FOR MINDFULNESS

- Stay neutral and objective.

- Continue to strengthen awareness by recognizing that thoughts are coming up—and that they are *only* thoughts.

- Maintain awareness of breathing.

The Flooding of Emotion

Lauren had a lot of trouble recalling what happened next. Eventually she remembered several images—of herself eating lunch alone in junior high, of sitting home on Fridays while her friends began to date, and of being too afraid to try out for a school play. These images came so quickly that they were merely flashes in her mind.

It was here that the amygdala began to hijack her experience. The images of earlier lonely experiences were triggered by the similar aloneness that Lauren experienced in the present.

FINDING THE POSSIBILITIES FOR MINDFULNESS

- Intentionally slow down the breath.

- Recognize what is happening; name it as flooding or being overwhelmed.

- Keep feeling the connection of your feet to the ground and focus also on the strength in your legs.

- Remember the stillness at the center of the storm; try to connect with the observing self.

The Entry of the Story Line

As Lauren remembered other times when she had felt excluded, her mind began to add to her long-standing belief that she would never belong. She practically heard the words "People don't like you. They think you are weird."

This is where the storm really took off. Thoughts, images, beliefs, and memories combined in a swirl to create a believable story about how things are and will probably remain. The story line is made up of sensations, thoughts, emotions, and inner commentary about the meaning of what is happening. This story line intensifies the already distressing emotions.

FINDING THE POSSIBILITIES FOR MINDFULNESS

- Direct awareness away from thinking, toward sensations in the body.

- Connect with the observing self: the part that is able to watch the thought stream and not get caught up in it.

- Remember that all experiences pass; this will not last forever.

The Urge to Escape from Feelings

Lauren got up and left the library. She stopped at the student union shop to buy a large bag of M&Ms. Part of her wanted to resist eating the candy, but she couldn't seem to help herself. Although she was focused on the sensations in her mouth, she didn't taste anything. Her world seemed to contract around the crunch of the candy.

At this point, the storm had taken over. Lauren reacted to the painful emotions as if they threatened her actual survival. The crunch of the candy and the sensations of melting chocolate distracted her from the intolerable feelings.

FINDING THE POSSIBILITIES FOR MINDFULNESS

- Direct awareness away from thinking to sensations in the body.

- Practice grounding in the body: notice strength in the legs and feet making contact with the floor.

- Remember that even this can be worked with.

Acting Out or Acting In

After she stopped crying, Lauren felt numb and drained of energy. She called herself names like "loser" and "pathetic." She was too tired to get back to writing her paper. She began to fear that she would flunk the class but felt like it wasn't worth the effort to try. The next day she still felt ashamed and wouldn't talk to Tiffany. When Tiffany asked her what was wrong, she wouldn't meet Tiffany's eyes, said, "Nothing," and turned away. Later she started a fight with Tiffany.

Lauren had now created two walls. One wall was between herself and her feelings. The self-aversion that she was experiencing was just too painful, so she had gone numb emotionally. Unfortunately, she still had enough energy to "act in": she continued to attack herself for a long list of flaws and mistakes. The second wall was between her and the outside world. She had become so disconnected from other people that she felt little for them but distrust and hostility—more aversion.

FINDING THE POSSIBILITIES FOR MINDFULNESS

- Do the Just a Minute Meditation (see chapter 6).

- Notice that the intensity of the storm experience has passed; things are different now.

- Remember that storms happen to everyone.

After-the-Storm Reflection

With reflection, Lauren was able to identify the triggers that had started the storm and the patterns of thought and feeling that added to its velocity. She was able to feel the loneliness and hurt that were magnified when she thought Tiffany was excluding her, but with the perspective of her mindful recollection, she wasn't overwhelmed by them. She had achieved a wise knowing about herself, and along with understanding came an unfamiliar feeling of compassion toward herself. She felt that the wisdom she gained in this reflection would help her avoid so much suffering the next time an emotional storm is triggered.

FINDING THE POSSIBILITIES FOR MINDFULNESS

- Even difficult experiences like emotional tsunamis have a beginning, middle, and end. Their pattern is predictable.

- Practice attending to feelings on a daily, even moment-to-moment basis.

- Recognize that storms are part of the human experience. Allow yourself to be human, too, and to learn what you can from these storms.

Tracking Your Own Storm

Find a place where you can comfortably sit and write. You might want to ask a good friend to be with you to help support your mindfulness. Sit for a few minutes simply focusing on your breathing. Then invite a memory of one of your emotional tsunamis into your mind. Begin with the first thing that comes to mind. Write about it under the appropriate category below. You don't have to begin at the beginning; you may even find it's easiest to start at the end of the storm and work backwards. It is also possible that the process of writing will help you to slow down and to fill in some of the gaps in your awareness. With patient attention, your memory may even supply you with more details about the experience. This experience is usually more like finding the pieces of a puzzle and putting them together than telling a straightforward story.

The Rising of Sensation

As you remember the storm, can you make contact with your body? Might it even be possible to remember the very first moments of tightening that took place somewhere in your body: perhaps in your neck or throat, your chest, your gut, or your face?

The Entry of Thought

What can you remember about the first thoughts? These will be thoughts that describe what was happening before you began to interpret the event.

What else?

Any more thoughts?

The Flooding of Emotion

Can you remember and describe the time when things seemed to speed up? Maybe there were images or flashes of old memories or maybe just words or phrases.

Anything else?

What emotions and sensations happened next? Maybe there was anger or a flash of heat in your body. Maybe there was sadness, and tears came to your eyes. Was there shame or embarrassment? How did they affect you?

The Entry of the Story Line

What did you tell yourself about what was happening?

What effect did the story line have on your feelings in the moment?

The Urge to Escape from Feelings

Was there a time when you thought, *I can't handle this?* What did you feel like doing?

Acting Out or Acting In

What did you do next?

Did you engage in any compulsive habits next? Did you light up a cigarette or start eating ice cream? Or something else?

Did you start criticizing yourself?

Did you start a fight with someone else?

After-the-Storm Reflection

Where were there possibilities for mindfulness? When might you have slowed things down? Was any damage done to you or your relationships? How can you repair it? Do you need to forgive yourself? Apologize to someone else?

End with a few minutes of the Just a Minute Meditation (see chapter 6).

FINDING THE SEEDS OF THE STORM

What makes it possible for our emotions to be triggered in this way? Why do some experiences become so overwhelming? Generally it is because our "small self" feels threatened in some way.

The small self is that part of us that is concerned for our protection and survival. It carries our personal stories, including all the ways that we think we are wrong or have been wronged by others. Whether these stories are true or not makes very little difference. When we get caught up in the stories or in the perceived threat to our small selves, it feels as if nothing else matters.

The small self believes that it is alone and separate from the rest of existence, so it is entirely focused on self-preservation. It believes itself to be weak and vulnerable and doesn't accept that being human means being vulnerable at times. Instead, the small self believes vulnerability is a sign of a deep flaw in its makeup. It believes that it must do everything possible to hide that flaw. When your small self feels threatened, you are at risk for an overwhelming emotional storm.

SMALL-SELF THREATS

The small self has a seemingly endless list of beliefs about what is flawed: *You're too fat. You don't have a degree. You don't know how to play politics like other people. People won't like you when they get to know you. You don't deserve as much as other people.* You can probably add several familiar ones to the list. Most of them arise from one of the following perceived threats:

Physical Survival	Sense of Significance	Sense of Belonging	Feeling of Scarcity
Fear I won't live through this.	**Fear** I don't really matter.	**Fear** If I'm too different, I won't be liked or loved.	**Fear** There is not enough (love, attention, food, money) to go around.
Belief The deeply held small-self belief is that emotional threats are *actually* life-threatening.	**Belief** Unless other people see, respect, approve of me, I don't really exist.	**Belief** If I don't figure out the rules to fitting in and follow them, I will be all alone.	**Belief** I have to compete for the good things of life.

Lauren's Example	**Lauren's Example**	**Lauren's Example**	**Lauren's Example**
Lauren felt flushed and dizzy, and had a hollow sense in her gut. Although she wasn't physically threatened, her brain didn't differentiate between physical and psychological threat.	Lauren felt overlooked and unimportant when Tiffany chose to spend time with other girls.	Lauren's fear that she would not make friends in college connected with long-standing fears that she was too different to ever really belong anywhere.	Lauren's fear that there wasn't enough love or affection to go around caused her to constantly compare what she had to what other people had.

How Do You Feel Threatened?

Review your example of an emotional tsunami and deepen your understanding of it by filling in the table below. Which of the following core threats were activated? What beliefs arose? How do they apply to what happened in your example? You may find that you are most vulnerable to one of the core threats or to several of them.

Physical Survival	Sense of Significance	Sense of Belonging	Feeling of Scarcity

Building a Raft

The previous exercises help support your mindfulness by bringing curiosity and reflection *after* the tsunami has struck and passed. These exercises help you build a life raft for the next storm. To add to your raft, review your writing and take a few more minutes to reflect on the following questions.

Are there situations where you are more likely to get caught up in a tsunami? Describe them.

_____

_____

_____

Are there people you find yourself more easily triggered by? Who are they? Do they have anything in common?

_____

_____

_____

What can you do to better prepare for these situations or people?

_____

_____

_____

Where in your experience might you have called upon mindfulness skills to slow the process down or lessen the harm?

_____

_____

_____

Improvising a Raft

It sometimes happens that a storm will drop you into a raging, flooding river before you have had time to build a sturdy raft. What if your partially built raft is sitting at the side of the river, and you see it as you rush by but can't get to it?

You may need to put a raft together out of the twigs and branches you can grab on to, and cling to that until the storm subsides. You have already learned some of the skills and beliefs you need. Improvising your raft under adverse conditions requires *RAW GRIT*.

RAW GRIT

Recognize what's happening	Call it what it is: a tsunami. Naming helps bring in the thinking brain.
Awareness	Notice as much about it as you can. When did it start? Where do you feel it in your body?
Wait it out	Recognize that when a storm takes hold it needs time to subside.
Ground yourself in the actual experience of the moment	Ask yourself, *What am I experiencing now? Can I stay present with it?* Direct whatever awareness you can to sensations in the body or to the breath.
Remember impermanence	Nothing lasts forever, not even difficulties.
Intention	Try to recall your intention to bring mindfulness to every situation possible.
Take refuge in others	Storms separate you from other people; do what you can to reconnect with someone safe.

Have you ever seen the aftermath of a tornado or hurricane? Although it may look as if the damage can never be repaired, within hours of the storm's ending, people are already clearing the wreckage. When the surface damage is cleaned up, what remains is the unharmed earth.

Similarly, with your own storms, there is a part of you that cannot be damaged. This is your "big self," the part of you that is connected to something larger—to the natural world, to the divine, to all of humanity. In the next chapters you will be guided to learn more about your big self and to learn practices to cultivate connection to it.

SUMMING UP CHAPTER 8

- Everyone is vulnerable to emotional storms.

- It is possible to grow in self-awareness by bringing mindfulness to the experience.

- The more identification there is with the small self and its beliefs, the more vulnerability there is to these storms.

- Skills can be developed that limit and even avoid the damage created by emotional storms.

Part 4

The Heart Pathways

Chapter 9

Connecting:

Come Home to Yourself

*The time will come
when, with elation,
you will greet yourself arriving
at your own door, in your own mirror
And each will smile at the other's welcome.*

Derek Walcott

The cultivation of a "good heart"—a heart that is open, accepting of self and others, generous, loving, and joyful—is the very core of the resilient life. In this chapter we begin walking the first of the heart pathways: the one that leads you home to the self you have forgotten or lost along the way, the self you have perhaps closed out of your heart.

The closing of your heart may have begun in a very forgotten moment—one in which you were hurt by a critical word or a cruel rejection. Over time you may have collected a great many supposed reasons why you are flawed, unworthy, broken, and in need of being fixed. Caught in the trap of self-rejection, you may have embarked on many self-improvement projects, all based on the belief that you are not good enough as you are.

We invite you to consider that you are good enough exactly as you are. We invite you to open your heart to yourself, and begin the path of deep healing from shame, self-rejection, and the pain of disconnection. In this chapter we offer you the chance to explore and repair your patterns of shutting yourself out of your own heart, and share practices that will help you reconnect with your essential goodness.

• Mary Ellen's Story: The Trap of Self-Rejection

Mary Ellen, a gracious and poised woman in her late fifties, said, "You could sum up my entire life in two words: 'report card.'" No part of Mary Ellen's performance escaped her own relentless scrutiny and judgment. She found fault with every aspect of herself, set impossibly high standards, and—in her eyes—never reached them. Though others saw her as creative, engaging, intelligent, and accomplished, she was caught in the trap of self-rejection. She could not see herself as anything other than inadequate, unlovable, and unworthy. She drove herself to great lengths to compensate for her sense of deficiency, striving beyond expectations at work and giving unselfishly of herself to her family and community. She amassed a library of self-help books, seeking in each one the path to self-improvement that would free her from the tyranny of the report card. Eventually she reached a breaking point. Unable to push herself any longer, she fell into a depressive episode, which generated more self-contempt and judgment.

At the root of Mary Ellen's self-rejection is toxic shame, that insidious and powerful emotional delusion that says *I am defective. I am not worthy. I am unlovable.*

Self-rejection divides you from yourself and from others. We believe that self-rejection and the shame at its root are primary causes of unhappiness and significant contributors to depression. We also believe that self-acceptance and healing from shame are possible, and that they open the door to a life of joy and resilience. This happens through healing the disconnection from self, through coming home to yourself.

THE PATHWAY OF SELF-ACCEPTANCE

Self-acceptance is a process, not an event. Although each person's path is unique, there are several key phases. You might find yourself cycling through them multiple times, as this is not a linear process.

Taking the First Step: Calling a Truce

Ending the inner war of self-rejection begins with calling a truce: setting the intention to befriend yourself. Rather than continuing to battle against herself, Mary Ellen opened her mind to the possibility that she could make peace with herself as she was and tear up the report card. This intention did not come easily, and it faded from time to time as the habitual ways of self-rejection cropped up again. With mindful acceptance she returned to the intention to befriend herself, and began again.

The Next Step: Connecting with the Rejected Self

Mary Ellen, like all who are caught in the trap of self-rejection, could see herself only through the eyes of her inner critic, who had nothing but contempt for her. On an intellectual level she realized her self-contempt was extreme and undeserved, but try as she might, she could not rid herself of the critical thoughts.

In fact it is impossible to shift from self-contempt to self-compassion simply through thinking about it; only the heart can generate the healing power of self-compassion. And before the heart can feel compassion, it is necessary to really see the suffering that is happening. If you are at a distance from your suffering, if shame and self-contempt have hardened you to it, your heart remains closed.

As Mary Ellen pondered these ideas, she told a story from her own experience that made this step of the process clearer to her. She lived in a large city and, on her way to work, often passed a woman at a traffic light, holding a sign that said "Homeless and desperate. Please give. God bless."

Seeing her from a distance, Mary Ellen hoped for a green light that would mean she could quickly pass by. When forced to stop at the intersection, she would avert her eyes, and her mind was filled with critical thoughts. Although some part of her was aware of the fact that she was judgmental and lacked understanding of the woman's plight, the critical part of her dominated those moments at the intersection. Every once in a while, as she was falling asleep, the woman's face appeared in Mary Ellen's mind. Over time, she began to fantasize about working at a homeless shelter, and eventually began volunteering, serving meals and listening to stories that gave her a deeper understanding of the woman she had so judged and turned away from. When she met the people in the shelter face to face and heard their stories, her heart spontaneously opened, and the judgments subsided.

Mary Ellen saw that she had been responding to herself just as she had responded to the homeless woman at the traffic light. She had turned her eyes away from herself and from the pain and shame that were at her core. She began to realize how many parts of herself she had turned away so that they were, in a sense, homeless. She invited these parts of herself into her awareness and began to understand the causes behind her self-rejection. She no longer sided with her inner critic and looked away, but turned toward her suffering self. As she did this, her heart began to open, and self-compassion appeared without effort.

The following exercise is designed to help you begin to see your own situation in more detail, with more clarity, so that your heart's door can begin to open to whatever parts of yourself you have rejected.

Guided Reflection: Connecting with Your Rejected Self

For this exercise, allow yourself some uninterrupted time, at least thirty minutes.

- With writing materials nearby, seat yourself comfortably, close your eyes, and invite your body to relax and soften. For a few minutes simply follow your breath, allowing your thoughts to settle.

- When you are ready, set the intention of connecting with the self that you have most rejected, that you struggle the most to accept. Allow a few minutes for an image of this rejected self to come to your mind's eye. Let it emerge in whatever way it does; there is no perfect or right way to do this.

- One way to come to see clearly what you have rejected is to use the following questions as a structure. Feel free to use them or to reflect and write in your own way to create an awareness of the parts of yourself that are in need of your healing attention. As you move through this reflection, you might find that your mind or heart contract and you want to move away. If this happens, simply return to your breath, and to the intention to open and see clearly.

What is it about my body that I have judged and rejected? Am I the wrong size? Color? Age?

_____

_____

_____

_____

_____

What is it about my mind that is not acceptable? Do I doubt my intelligence? Am I critical of my tendencies toward depressed or anxious thoughts? Do I judge some of my thoughts as "bad"?

_____

_____

_____

_____

_____

What about my emotional self? Have I rejected some or all of my feelings? Do I judge myself for struggling with blue moods or fear or jealousy? Do I blame myself for my feelings? Or condemn myself because of my anger or irritability?

_____

_____

_____

_____

_____

How have I judged and condemned my choices or actions? Are there choices or actions I have not forgiven myself for?

_____

_____

_____

_____

_____

Is there anything else about myself that I have judged harshly, any part of me that is suffering that pain of rejection?

_____

_____

_____

_____

- When you have finished writing this inventory, close your eyes and change your focus to the breath and the sensations in your body. Notice them with mindfulness, with as much unconditional acceptance and kindness as possible. You may begin to really feel the pain of being so harshly judged or rejected. As you do, open as much as you can to how this feels, and notice any spark of compassion that appears.

- Let your breath carry warmth and healing to the areas of your body that feel any distress. Invite yourself to soften, and remember your intention to move toward a new relationship with yourself—a relationship of love and acceptance.

- Remember that this process of connecting with the pain of your rejected self may take time, and know that you can return to this experience again and again.

THE HEALING POWER OF MINDFULNESS

Once you have taken stock of what you have rejected, and have begun to feel some compassion for your own suffering, you are ready to more deeply explore the healing power of mindfulness. The following meditation is one way to access the deeper resources you have access to: your own loving and compassionate energy. This is a meditation we encourage you to practice again and again.

Guided Meditation: Healing the Rejected Self

For this guided meditation, select from the previous exercise one of the parts of yourself that has been rejected and that you feel ready to open to. For your first experience with this meditation, don't select the part of you that holds the most shame.

- Seat yourself comfortably, in a relaxed but alert position. Focus for several minutes on your breath, inviting the mind to settle. Let go with each exhalation.

- Be aware of the sensations in your body as they are now, without judging. Invite any tense parts of your body to relax, to soften. Be aware of thoughts as they drift through, and your emotional state at this moment.

- Invite into your awareness, into this space, someone you trust who cares for you, who completely accepts you as you are. This could be someone you know: a teacher, mentor, or friend. It might be an animal: a loving pet. It could even be someone you only know of, such as a spiritual teacher. It is some being who gives you a sense that you are completely acceptable and lovable, just as you are. Sense this other being right here, close by, looking at you with eyes that really express caring.

- Create an intention to let that caring in, even if you feel resistance. Open your heart as widely as you can to this loving energy. You might wish to put your hand over your heart, gently warming and inviting it to soften.

- When you are ready, invite an image of the rejected part of yourself that is in need of healing to appear. Create this image in as much detail as possible, including visual appearance, emotions and thoughts you have about it. Perhaps you can see the situations in which it appears, what you believe about this part of yourself, or the way that you think others see it. Spend several minutes with this image. If your attention wanders, simply bring it back to the breath and the image.

- In this moment, set an intention in your heart and mind to open to this part of yourself that is in need of your compassionate attention. Seek to befriend it.

- As you focus on this rejected part of yourself, notice any sensations in your body that are triggered. Where do you notice the sensations? What type of sensations are they? Aching, tingling, heavy, cold, hot, prickly, dull, sharp? Are they moving or staying in one place? Are there names for these sensations: sadness, disgust, grief, fear, repulsion, shame, anger, others? Naming and noticing are powerful ways to connect with what you have rejected.

- As you note any resistance, any tendency to shut down or push away these sensations, recall the spirit of mindfulness: nonjudging, open, and friendly curiosity. Open your mind and heart to yourself, allowing any and all of these sensations to unfold exactly as they do. Continue to open and soften as you explore the painful places in need of your attention and compassion.

- You may find that the inner critic shows up; in that case know that it's possible to open in a nonjudging way even to that part of yourself, which also carries pain.

- If the suffering becomes too intense, simply return to the place of safety and invite the loving presence of the compassionate other to be here with you right now. If this is difficult, no problem. Take your time and continue to invite that loving presence to appear. See those eyes, looking at you with acceptance and love. Let this caring surround you and fill the space around you. Breathe it in and let it touch you in the place of deepest pain, flowing around and through in a soothing way.

- Continue breathing, and allowing whatever is unfolding in you to be held in this space of loving presence and compassion that is flowing around and through you.

- As you do this, listen carefully to this suffering part of yourself. What might it need from you in order to heal? Is there a kindness you can offer yourself? A word? An affirmation? If so, offer it in the spirit of compassion and healing.

- Spend as much time as you need, connecting in this loving way with the self you have rejected. Know that this process may need to be repeated again and again, and that's perfectly all right. This source of compassion is available to you at any time. It only requires you to mindfully open your heart to yourself.

CREATING A SELF-ACCEPTING LIFE

Even as the healing process continues, you may create new ways of being with yourself that come from a place of self-acceptance, rather than the old ways of self-rejection. This self-accepting life begins with remembering who you really are and can be.

Begin with a Vision

In the mid-1950s, near Bangkok, a community of Buddhist monks was told that they would have to relocate because a new highway was being built through their land. The most challenging part of the move was the transport of their temple's Buddha figure, which towered over ten feet high and weighed several tons. It was a simple figure made of clay, nothing elaborate, but it was of value to these monks because it had been in the community for centuries. So they arranged to have workmen bring equipment to their site to accomplish the move.

The story goes that just as the Buddha figure was lifted from the ground, it began to crack in several places, alarming the monks. They ordered the project to stop for the day until larger equipment could be brought in, and because it was beginning to rain, they covered the statue with a tarp and went to sleep. One of the monks, unable to sleep, took it on himself to stand watch overnight. He checked on the statue every hour or so, wanting to make sure that the cracks were not deepening. As he shined his flashlight over the surface, he saw small glimmers of light. Moving closer, he noticed that there appeared to be something under that clay surface, and he went to fetch a hammer and chisel. He carefully chipped away at the clay, and to his amazement there appeared a layer of gold. He called his fellow monks, who all came with their tools, and soon they had uncovered a solid gold Buddha figure.

Historians believe that this statue was created in the fourteenth or fifteenth century, and that it had been covered in plaster at some point to hide its value from the invading Burmese army. Those who had done this had died long before, and the secret of the true nature of the statue had died with them. Now the truth was revealed, and the statue can be seen today at the Wat Traimit temple in Bangkok's Chinatown. It weighs five tons and is made of solid gold. It is truly priceless.

Your Golden Self

Over the years, your golden essence, so obvious early in your life, may have been covered with layers of "plaster"—criticism, comparisons, expectations, stories about your unworthiness—until you lost connection with your essential self.

This exercise is intended to help you reconnect with that essential self and restore your relationship with it. Allow yourself plenty of quiet time for this experience, at least thirty minutes.

1. Seated in a comfortable place, with your writing materials nearby, prepare yourself for a period of reflection on your life.

2. Begin by quieting your mind, focusing on your breath, and relaxing your body.

3. After a few minutes, begin to open your storehouse of memories. Search through these memories to find a time—a moment, a few hours, a day—when you recall feeling most completely yourself, most completely alive or free from self-consciousness and comparison with others. This could be a childhood memory, or it could be from the more recent past. Give yourself plenty of time to find one that feels right to you. (Note: If you have difficulty doing this, try this exercise again on another day, and talk with someone who knows you well and can help you think it through or share her own examples in a way that prompts your memory.)

Reconstruct this time in your mind's eye with as much specific detail as you can. Where were you? What were you involved in doing? Who was with you? What do you recall about your emotions at the time? What else do you remember?

_____

_____

_____

_____

_____

_____

_____

_____

_____

_____

_____

_____

_____

_____

_____

_____

_____

_____

When you've completed this writing, reflect back over it and find three or four words that capture the experience. You might choose to share this story with another, and have that person reflect back the words that come to mind as you talk. Examples might be single words, such as "free," "strong," "courageous," "connected." Or you might choose simple phrases, such as "free from fear," physically strong," "alive and well," "loved and accepted."

_____

_____

_____

_____

_____

_____

_____

Savor this experience. The self you recall in this experience is your golden self: your essence, the truth about who you are and can be. You will be using the phrases you've just written as the basis for creating a new relationship with yourself, one that is characterized by befriending and wishing all good things for yourself.

PRACTICE LOVING-KINDNESS FOR YOURSELF

Loving-kindness meditation is a 2,600-year-old practice of wishing for self and others the things we all desire most: health, well-being, happiness, peace of mind, and so on. In its traditional format, the practice is done during seated meditation, and consists of a series of three or four statements expressing these positive intentions, repeated again and again, in harmony with the breath. This traditional set of wishes is one example:

May I be filled with loving-kindness.
May I be well in body and in mind.
May I be peaceful and at ease.
May I be happy.

The meditation begins with the focus on self, where it may need to remain for a long time. Eventually the wishes are extended to those we love, those we are acquainted with, those we have difficulty with, and, ultimately, all beings. It is a profound practice that has great impact on the heart's capacity for compassion. It also creates a sense of social connection and support, increasing life satisfaction and reducing symptoms of depression.

The Benefits of Loving-Kindness Meditation

The practice of loving-kindness meditation appears to be related to the reduction of depressive symptoms and greater overall life satisfaction. In 2008, Barbara L. Fredrickson and colleagues at the University of North Carolina at Chapel Hill, along with colleagues from the University of Michigan, published results of a study in which approximately half of the 139 adult participants were randomly assigned to the practice of loving-kindness meditation, and half were not. Those who practiced the meditation reported increases over time in their experience of positive emotions, as well as mindfulness, sense of purpose, and social connection. These factors were shown to be predictive of decreased depressive symptoms and a greater overall degree of happiness.

As part of healing from shame and self-rejection, we suggest that you practice the beginning phase of the loving-kindness meditation: the phase focused on yourself. Using the three or four key words or phrases you identified in the previous exercise, create your own set of wishes. Using the words in the example given above, for instance, the wishes would be:

May I be free from fear.

May I be strong.

May I feel alive and well.

May I feel loved and accepted.

When you have finished developing your own phrases, you might wish to write them on a small card. They will form the heart of your work with the loving-kindness meditation that follows.

Loving-Kindness Meditation for Self

- Begin this meditation by settling yourself in a comfortable position, alert yet relaxed. Take a few moments to scan your body for any sensations of tension and invite them to relax and soften.

- Focus for several minutes simply on your breath as it enters and leaves the body, inviting your mind to settle and quiet.

- Now focus particularly on the breath as you sense it in your heart center, perhaps placing your hand gently on that part of your body. Sense the coming and going of the breath there, and any other sensations you notice. Be aware of how open your heart center is at this moment, and mindfully, without judging, invite it to open a bit more.

- Invite into your awareness the image of a compassionate other: a person who accepts you unconditionally and wishes you well. This could be someone you know or only know of: a teacher, mentor, friend, a spiritual teacher. It might be an animal: a loving pet. Sense this other being close to you, looking at you with eyes that really express those loving wishes for your happiness.

- Allow your heart to open to the loving wishes this person has for you. If you find yourself contracting or shutting this loving energy out, simply breathe and open again, to whatever degree you can. Spend a few minutes just allowing your heart to be filled with this sense of loving care.

- Now invite into your awareness an image of your own self. This may be yourself at this present time or at some earlier time in your life. Invite that self to sit down across from you, and observe as much detail about yourself as you can: your body, your posture, your face. Sense how it feels to be right here with yourself.

- Now, moving awareness again to your heart center, open your heart and invite that image of yourself into the circle of loving energy that is there. Sense your heart holding and deeply connecting with yourself in this moment. If you find any sense of contraction, simply breathe and remind yourself of your loving intention to open.

- Now, with heartfelt sincerity, repeat your loving-kindness phrases silently, again and again, in rhythm with your breathing. As you repeat your phrases, you might find that you wish to change them slightly, or even leave out or add some. Feel free to do this until you feel that they are exactly what you wish for yourself from your most loving heart.

- Repeat these phrases for as long as you wish. As you move toward ending this meditation, return to your breath for just a few minutes, noting the feelings and sensations present now. Be grateful for this experience, whatever you have found it to be.

It's important to note again that the practice of loving-kindness for self is the foundation of a practice that eventually moves beyond the self. As you extend loving wishes for happiness and well-being to all, you create a powerful antidote to the isolation and self-absorption that depression often brings.

Freed from ruminating on your own deficiencies, you can now give your attention to others and share yourself more fully with them. This is the foundation of belonging, which we will turn to in the next chapter.

SUMMING UP CHAPTER 9

- Self-rejection and shame are key contributors to recurrent depression.

- Healing from the wounds of self-rejection is possible through connection with your own suffering and the spontaneous arising of compassion that is its natural outcome.

- When cultivated intentionally, self-compassion and loving-kindness help heal the disconnection that self-rejection has created.

- You have within you a self that is free and whole, perfect just as it is.

Chapter 10

Belonging:

Create Circles of Connection

We can live without religion and meditation, but we cannot survive without human affection.

The Dalai Lama

"I know I sound like a typical older person when I say that things were better when I was a kid, but at least in this way, they were: I remember summer mornings when I would jump out of bed, throw on my clothes, and dash out the back door. I can still hear the sound of the screen door slamming behind me as I ran out to look for my friends. And I always found them; there was always someone to play with. The mornings started on the swing set and ended with hide-and-seek as nighttime came on. Of course, it wasn't perfect. I remember getting into fights and being jealous when a friend played with someone else more than with me, but it all just seemed to flow from fun to fight and back to fun again."

Is Mary remembering a golden age that never was? Or are these memories a resource for her, a time of unquestioned belonging that motivates her to continue to seek out meaningful connections—even though it seems harder now than it did back then?

No matter what you are experiencing right now in your life, you can be certain that in your early years, there were enough people who knew you and liked you and cared for you. You may think that there weren't many—but there were *enough*. You received enough attention and love to survive. Now you would like to do more than survive. You would like to *belong*. No matter how discouraging relationships have been for you, it is still possible to create a circle of belonging.

CIRCLES OF BELONGING

- ## *Mary's Story*

Mary now lives in a townhouse where she knows a few neighbors but only knows them well enough to nod to them. She works for a large insurance company, where she arrives early every morning. Once she sits down in her cube and opens her computer, she barely looks up till noon. Occasionally she will take a walk with a coworker through the corridors and staircases of her office building, but more often she eats a solitary lunch as she continues to work at her desk.

On her way home from work, Mary stops at a fitness club three nights a week. She doesn't know anyone at the club, and she hurries through her routine, saving her shower until she gets home. Once home, she turns on her TV for company and listens for an hour or more to news of disasters and threats from around the world.

How can Mary not be lonely? And how much does this social starvation contribute to her depression? Of course, Mary is aware that she feels lonely, but the reasons for those feelings became much clearer to her after she made two contrasting maps. Called *circle of belonging* maps, they are a tool that provides a picture of a person's social connections. Mary completed one for her early years and one for her current life. When she saw how much richer her early networks had been, she began to wonder how she could add to her circle in the present. Later in this chapter, you will be given details about completing a circle of belonging map for yourself.

Mary's Childhood Circle of Belonging

Mr. Halley (principal), mailman, friends' parents, people at church

Grandma Betty and Grandpa Al, Mrs. Parker (teacher), Peter, Candy and Mimi (friends), baby sister Kari, Marie the baby-sitter, cousins Tracy and Mark

Mom, Dad, Grandma Mayme, Grandpa Jim, big brother Joe, Susie, Pam, and Sandra (friends), Anni the dog, cousins Cherly and Laurie, Pastor Bob

Mary

Mary's Current Circle of Belonging

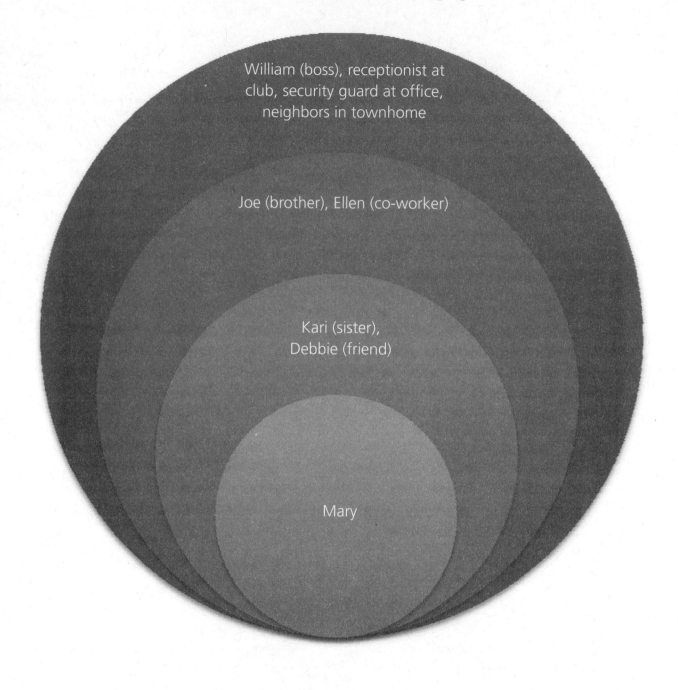

William (boss), receptionist at club, security guard at office, neighbors in townhome

Joe (brother), Ellen (co-worker)

Kari (sister), Debbie (friend)

Mary

THE SPIRAL OF SEPARATION

As an infant Mary knew nothing about separation. A newborn does not experience a self that is inside her skin and a world that is outside of it. It is only gradually that humans develop a sense of individuality, of being a separate self, the belief that "I" exist apart from others. This awareness of being a self is what makes humans different from other creatures. It is what allows you to feel like "yourself."

The sense of separateness comes with both blessings and curses. It allows you to develop as an individual and to be uniquely yourself, but it is a limited experience of reality. Although you feel separate, there are many ways that you are connected to something larger. It is as if you were really a hand but sensed yourself to be only a finger. As a finger, you could point things out and you could cooperate with other fingers to pick things up, but there would always be a feeling of being apart.

Spiritual traditions tell us that in our deepest essence, we are hands, not fingers, that we are in fact interconnected and unified with each other and with the larger universe to which we belong. Albert Einstein described our belief that we are separate as "an optical delusion of consciousness" (as quoted in Calaprice 2005, 4). We are both/and: both separate individuals *and* interconnected parts of a whole. Problems arise when *all* we see is our separateness.

What are the consequences of this delusion of separation?

- We identify with our small self.

- We feel alone.

- We feel threatened.

- We feel competitive.

- We feel anxious and afraid.

This delusion is so widely shared that most people live their lives as if it were true. And so, for all intents and purposes, it becomes true. Under such conditions, many people experience a gnawing sense of insecurity that they can't really name or explain.

Fortunately, there are things you can do to challenge the delusion. You can find ways to create community and to participate with others in caring and generous ways. You can appreciate all of the ways that you are interdependent with others, all of the times that cooperation works. You can seek out evidence that you are more like than different from other people and so find ways to connect—not just safely, but with joy.

IS MY UNIVERSE FRIENDLY?

Einstein also said that one of the most important questions a human being can ask is this: "Is the universe friendly?" (as quoted in Oyle 1979, 163). Your answer to that question depends a great deal upon the degree to which you feel a sense of belonging.

The following questionnaire will help you identify how satisfied you feel with the amount of social support—how much sense of belonging—you experience. It is important to remember that people desire different amounts of connection; one person may be content with a good friend or two, and another person feels alone unless there is daily contact with several people. It is also important to remember that the presence of depression has a strongly negative influence on how separate we perceive ourselves to be. You might want to answer these questions at two different times, once when depression is present and another time when you are freer from it.

Belonging Questionnaire

For each question below, circle the number that is most true for you:

1—Hardly ever

2—Some of the time

3—As often as not

4—Most of the time

5—Nearly always

My circle of belonging is as full as I'd like it to be.	1 2 3 4 5
I'm part of a group or groups where I share values with the other members.	1 2 3 4 5
There is always someone I feel I can talk to about what is important to me.	1 2 3 4 5
I have many outlets where I can share my personal gifts.	1 2 3 4 5
When I approach a new situation, I feel confident I will be welcomed.	1 2 3 4 5
I am good at reading people's nonverbal messages.	1 2 3 4 5
I seldom feel dissatisfied with my relationships.	1 2 3 4 5
I have people in my life who see my strengths and vulnerabilities and still appreciate me.	1 2 3 4 5
I have people in my life who want good things for me.	1 2 3 4 5
There is more about me that is like other people than is different from them.	1 2 3 4 5

Understanding Your Scores

41–50: a strong and healthy sense of belonging.

31–40: a satisfactory sense of belonging.

21–30: an unsatisfactory sense of belonging.

10–20: at this time in your life, you experience a very low sense of belonging.

Your Circle of Belonging

Another way to measure your quality of belonging is to fill in your current circle of belonging. The center represents you, of course, and the widening circles represent your network of social connection. First are those in your inner ring, whom you feel safe and at ease with. These are the people you talk to about what is important to you: problems, dreams, wishes, and so forth. In the next ring you can place people for whom you have feelings of affection and friendliness but haven't let into the inner ring. The final ring should contain people you see with some regularity, whom you would recognize on the street, for example, but whom you interact with minimally. It is possible that some family members belong in this circle.

Now that you have filled in your circle, are there rings where you would like to have more people?

_____

_____

Are there people you would like to move into a closer ring? _____

_____

What is one small thing you could do today to enrich your circle? _____

_____

_____

THE COSTS OF LONELINESS

"Loneliness" is the word given to the pain you feel when you are cut off from your relationships—when there are too few of them or when the quality of them disappoints you. Loneliness often intensifies when depression is present, due in part to lack of motivation to reach out to others. It may also be hard to believe that other people want to be around you if you have rejecting feelings toward yourself: *I don't even want to be with myself; how can I believe that anyone else wants to be with me?*

Experts agree social isolation is bad for health. An analysis of forty-eight studies looking at social relationships and mortality suggests that social isolation increases the risk of death as much as smoking or obesity. An interesting point from the study is that social relationships should be taken as seriously as other risk factors that affect mortality (Holt-Lunstad, Smith, and Layton 2010).

We all know that loneliness is painful. Have you ever felt rejected by someone and felt that you were in actual physical pain? A recent study confirms your experience. This study looked at brain activity after rejection and made a remarkable finding: the part of the brain activated by rejection is the very same part that is activated by a burn injury, one of the most painful physical traumas one can experience (Kross et al. 2011).

If you are someone who has a low sense of belonging, or who feels isolated and cut off from others, you probably don't need to read about studies that confirm what you already know: loneliness hurts both the body and the spirit. What you may not realize is the power of connection to heal.

There are four known factors that promote healthy, well-connected neurons: diet, exercise, mental stimulation, and social connection. Of these factors, it is social connection that has the most powerful benefits (Strasser et al. 2006). If a healthy sense of belonging can encourage the creation of new brain cells, and help them grow and connect better with other brain cells, then it can also help you recover from depression. It is a powerful means of sustaining your recovery and moving you toward an experience of joy.

Create a Vision of Belonging

You may be thinking, *Oh, great, another thing I'm not doing right, another way I'm making my life worse.* If you are having such thoughts, please invite your inner critic to leave the room. In fact, if you can remember back to chapter 2, where we talked about the inner visionary, now would be a good time to invite that part of yourself to join the conversation.

In the guided imagery below, you will align with your inner visionary to begin creating a new vision for yourself, as if you were creating the blueprint for building a house of belonging.

The Belonging Vision

- Settle into your comfortable, alert, and upright position, bringing your body to a position that supports your ability to direct your attention and bring awareness to your breath.

- After a few minutes of mindful breathing, direct your awareness to your body. Feel the connection of your feet to the floor…the contact of parts of your body with the chair or cushion…noticing any areas of stiffness or holding and inviting them to relax.

- Bring attention now to your heart center, that part of your chest around the breastbone… checking in with your heart center…inviting the heart to open…soften …feel warmth.

- In partnership with your inner visionary, let yourself feel your desire to belong, to feel safe and welcome, recognized and wanted. If it has been a long time since you have had such an experience, there may be some grief about its absence. If so, that's all right; just allow the grief, knowing it comes out of the deep human desire for connection.

- Still working with your inner visionary, call up a scene in your life where you felt awkward and shy, uncertain of your welcome. This could be with a group of strangers…or some friends that you have come to feel insecure with…or maybe with a partner or spouse if some distance has come between you.

- Now, invite your heart to open to the others in the scene. See if it's possible to experience a greater sense of ease. … In this moment, for just this moment, letting go of the obstacles to belonging…the painful memories, the fear of rejection, the worry about being accepted… let them all go and feel, for just this moment, the delight of a heart that is open to others, that knows it can be both welcomed and welcoming.

- Allow yourself to rest in the moment…feeling the absence of stress and the presence of *ease.*

- In a few moments, thank your inner visionary for showing you what your heart longs for and for showing you what can be.

CONNECTING BY ENGAGING BODY, MIND, AND HEART

The suffering of loneliness, like all suffering, can be reduced by identifying and working with the second arrows that intensify it. As you may recall from chapter 6, "second arrows" refer to the ways that suffering is compounded by our resistance to what is, and through unhelpful ways of thinking, reacting, and acting. Just as the sensation of pain intensifies when muscles contract around an injury, the emotional pain of loneliness intensifies when the heart contracts around the pain of separation.

The remainder of this chapter will offer you ways of strengthening your connections and thereby lessening the pain of loneliness.

Connecting through the Body

As you may remember from reading about the stress response at the beginning of this workbook, the body is exquisitely reactive to danger and responds immediately and thoroughly to anything it assesses as a threat. There has been a great deal of research done about the stress response, and no doubt you have learned a lot about its negative impact on health. But you have probably not heard as much about another brain response, one that is far more positive in its effects. This is called the *oxytocin response* or the tend-and-befriend response.

Under certain conditions, the brain releases the hormone oxytocin. Also known as the "cuddle hormone," it is like a wonder drug for connection. When it is released, people feel a sense of closeness and connection. Oxytocin is involved in all the processes that help us to relax and delight in the presence of others. It works to increase trust, reduce fear, and deepen empathy. This hormone is triggered when the body is most united with another person—as during childbirth, nursing, and sexual intimacy. However, it doesn't take such grand experiences to benefit from the oxytocin response.

As you read through the following list of activities, identify which ones are available to you and which ones you could add to your life. Each of them can trigger the oxytocin response.

- Greet someone with a hug.

- Share a sweet kiss.

- Stroke the fur of a pet.

- Remember a time when you received something that pleased you.

- Remember a time when you gave someone something that made them happy.

- Root for your team, especially with a group of other fans.

- Create music in a group by joining a band, choir, or orchestra.

- Write about your greatest values and principles.

Another option is to start behaving like someone who is already connected to others. Although we usually speak of belonging as a feeling, it is also possible to practice belonging behaviors—to act as if you already belong. For example, you can try:

- Making eye contact with a person you pass in the school hallway or office corridor

- Giving someone the kind of compliment that lets him know you've *seen* him

- Letting your face and eyes soften

- Inviting a gentle smile to your lips

- Initiating a greeting

You might have spent your life so far in the waiting role: waiting to be invited, waiting to be selected. It might even seem inauthentic of you to offer an invitation. *After all*, you might be thinking, *If I am uncomfortable doing something, doesn't it mean I'm not being real?* The answer to that is a resounding no. In learning any new skill, it takes time to build confidence and comfort. And it's fine to be a bit awkward as you learn. After all, the first time you tried to walk, you fell right over. Even if you have held back until now, this is something you can begin to alter right away.

Connecting through the Mind

Your brain is doing one of its most important jobs—scanning for danger—when it divides people into two groups: them and us. Your thoughts and beliefs play a major role in how you decide which group someone new belongs to and whether or not you decide to pursue more contact with that person. Thoughts and beliefs that grow out of a sense of separation set people up to think of others as potential threats instead of as possible friends or allies. Cultivating thoughts that encourage you to see more people as potential members of your tribe can help you to be more open to others. The more open you are to others, the richer is your circle of belonging.

It is helpful to challenge your automatic judgments and ways of thinking about other people. The following example is an invitation to start the day in a new way.

Imagine getting up in the morning knowing that it is a day that has been especially orchestrated for you. Every single person that you encounter today has been specifically chosen to offer you a gift—a lesson, an insight, a challenge, a difficulty—and each of these gifts shares this purpose: to remind you that you are not alone and to wake you up to your true nature, the part of you that is and has always been completely safe.

How would your day unfold if you knew this to be true?

_____

_____

Try bringing this mind-set into your day's first encounter with another person.

OPENING YOUR CIRCLES

What requirements do you bring to new encounters? Do you approach new people with a sense of open curiosity? Or do you make up your mind about some people before you even interact with them? In many cases a potential connection is dismissed before it even has a chance to begin. If we hold fewer requirements for entry into our circles, we can also have greater variety and richness in our connections. For example, consider Ellen's experience in a small town in northern Minnesota.

- ## *Ellen's Story*

"I've always been someone who really likes 'deep' discussions. I was asking about the meaning of life back in junior high. I scoffed at people who got into rooting for the football team or decorating for prom. I thought they were frivolous. In Minnesota everyone talks about the weather all the time. I refused to join in. Again, I thought they were being shallow. I only liked to talk about feelings and meaning. I guess it's no surprise that I became a psychologist. Early in my career, I had to move away from the Cities to a small town of eight thousand people. Because I worked at a mental health center with other therapists, I was able to have the deep talks I loved. But a funny thing happened up there. The town is set in the north woods, and almost everyone heated with a wood-burning stove. I decided it was a romantic idea, so after a few mishaps, I learned how to operate my own stove. This opened up a new world for me—the world of wood. I call what happened there learning to 'talk wood.' I learned to talk about full cords and fireplace cords, mixed hardwoods and the proper length of time to season the wood. It turned out to be a nearly universal language and opened up so many conversations for me. And, of course, it often led to more personal conversations about other topics. I still love to talk wood, and when I burn a properly seasoned maple log in the fireplace, its fragrance takes me right back to that community and the connections I made there."

What requirements might you be imposing on people before you talk with them? _____

_____

How do you want them to look or dress? _____

_____

Do their religious and political beliefs have to match yours? _____

_____

How open are you to other people's education level and type of employment? _____

_____

What people are you most likely to write off based on first impressions? _____

_____

Write about a time when you realized that your initial judgment about someone was incorrect. _____

_____

_____

If you wanted to, where might you begin to relax your requirements? _____

_____

_____

ONE-MINUTE COMMUNITIES

Close, lifelong friendships and family relationships add depth and richness to our lives, but they are not the only opportunities for pleasurable and meaningful connection. Friendships that go back to grade school exist at one end of the connection spectrum. One-minute communities exist at the other. You can experience a minute community…in a minute. They happen in moments like when you are standing in a grocery line or commenting about a book to someone else who is browsing in a bookstore. They don't have to be relationships that are going to go somewhere. They are already here. Although brief, they can create a connection glow that lasts for several hours. They can open your heart.

Connecting through the Heart

Buddhist teacher Pema Chödrön offers a beautiful way to think about the human heart. She compares it to a sea anemone. The sea anemone has a hole at its top, which is open to receive the food that its ocean home provides. However, when the anemone is shocked or startled in some way, it automatically closes its opening. This protects the tender creature within the shell, but also means that it gets no nourishment despite being immersed in it.

In the same way, the human heart can open to receive nurturing in the form of love and connection. And it can shut down instinctively in response to a threat or scare. It is particularly vulnerable to shutting down when we experience a hurt from another person. Although it is natural to move toward self-protection, the human heart that is habitually shut down can forget to open up again. The following practice encourages you to remember to open.

Heart-Opening Meditation

- Whether your heart feels wide open or long closed off, it is possible to invite openness into it.

- Begin by sitting quietly in a position that supports alertness and allows ease…focus on the rhythmic inhaling and exhaling of your breathing.

- After a few moments, invite your mind to quiet and your breath to deepen and slow…gently filling and emptying.

- Now place the palm of one hand over your heart center—on the chest just over the breastbone…focus your awareness on that part of you…does it feel tight and hard like a stone… warm and open like a sun-filled window…fluttering like a bird…or some other way? However you find it, invite your heart to open just a bit, to warm and soften, to relax in the warmth of the breath.

- Stay with this practice for a few minutes, just directing the breath to the heart center, inviting feelings of warmth deep into the heart…perhaps thinking the words, *welcome, you are welcome here*.

- After a comfortable amount of time, thank yourself for being willing to try this experience.

- Even if it feels as if nothing is happening, the act of directing attention to the heart center is an invitation for it to warm and soften, to regain its ability to welcome life in.

GENEROSITY: THE GREAT ANTIDOTE TO ISOLATION

Have you ever experienced the joy of giving or receiving just the right thing? Have you felt your heart warm and expand as it is touched by the gift? Having been on the giving end and the receiving end, have you noticed how similar they feel? According to the Buddha, a generous act dissolves the small self. With no thought of reward by the giver and with no debt incurred by the receiver, a generous act changes the world from one of isolation to one of connection. It is a temporary world, of course, but one that can be remembered and savored in lonely times. In the world of generosity, your gain is my pleasure, your happiness gives me happiness. In the world of generosity, your success doesn't threaten or diminish mine. It is a world that can be called into being by any act of giving.

Cultivating a Generous Heart

- Sit quietly in a comfortable position as you focus on your breath. Allow your mind to settle.

- Place your attention on your heart center, noticing whatever feeling is there at this moment and accepting it just as it is.

- Bring to mind someone who has recently received some very good news. When you have created a clear image of this person, muster as much generosity as you can.

- Silently offer this person a phrase such as:

  May your happiness grow and be with you always.

  May your success continue.

  Your joy gives me joy.

- Notice how this feels. If you have any resistance to this, just open to it and remember your intention to cultivate a generous heart.

- If you'd like, you can call up the image of another person who is experiencing some special goodness right now and repeat the same phrases to this person.

- Be generous with yourself if this is difficult, perhaps directing the same phrases to your own heart:

  May my happiness grow and always be with me.

  May my success continue.

  May I share in everyone's joy.

- When you feel finished with this process, bring your awareness back to the breath for a minute or two.

- Remember these phrases and this intention throughout the day, silently offering it to those you encounter.

LISTENING WITH A WIDE-OPEN HEART

One of the key ingredients to connection is to be able to listen deeply to others. The gift of true listening is one of the most generous gifts you can offer someone.

There is a story of a town that had a small-town heroes contest. Imagine the surprise of the townspeople when the contest was won by a five-year-old boy who had been nominated by his elderly neighbor. When he was interviewed for a story for the local newspaper and asked what he had done, his reply was short and sweet: "Well, Mr. Larson was sad when Mrs. Larson died, so I just sat on his lap and let him cry."

Have you ever had an experience with someone who was so completely present and so fully accepting of you that your shy inner self felt safe enough to come forth and be heard? Is this something you have been able to offer to someone else? If so, you've had an experience of deep listening, of being listened to with an unobstructed heart.

Deep Listening Exercise

Take a moment now to think of a time when you were listened to in this way. Close your eyes, allow your mind to settle, and go back in time until your memory lights upon a scene when someone listened deeply to you. If you can't think of any such time, just imagine it, knowing that for most of us, these are rare experiences.

What were the circumstances in your life at the time?

_____

_____

_____

Who was listening to you, and what was it about them that allowed you to open up to them?

_____

_____

_____

What did it feel like to reveal your self so fully to another?

_____

_____

_____

What do you think they saw in you that you couldn't see in yourself?

_____

Who are the people in your life, now or in the past, who really listen to you?

_____

_____

_____

It is a great gift to be listened to so deeply. It doesn't happen often, because it requires certain qualities on the part of the listener that seem to be in short supply: a calm mind with steady attention, an open heart with nonjudging acceptance, a deeply connected presence with compassionate awareness.

Listening well comes naturally to some, but it can also be practiced. Below are some of the skills to practice when you listen to others, or to look for in a skilled listener whom you'd like to have in your life.

The Skills of Deep Listening

Focus all your attention on the speaker. See the other person as whole and innocent, doing the best she can at any given moment; she doesn't need to be "fixed." You don't need to figure things out for her. Allow the other person to come to her own truths, trusting that she has all that she needs within.

Let the other person speak freely. Just listen, allowing her words to sink into you. You don't need to respond. If you do speak, speak from the heart, saying only what is true for *you*. Ask only a few open, honest questions—those that encourage the other person to speak more deeply—questions to which you don't think you already know the answers.

Allow emotions to arise naturally with no need to comfort or try to stop the emotion. Feel comfortable with silence and allow for periods in which no words are spoken. Hold the other person with openness, compassion, and acceptance.

These are the very qualities that you have been developing through this workbook, and that you can continue to grow into throughout your life. So even if you can't think of a single time when you have been deeply heard, or a single person who really listens to you, you can do this for others. In doing so, you are also creating the conditions for having more people with these qualities in *your* life.

SUMMING UP CHAPTER 10

- Connection is a human birthright.

- Loneliness is a call to connection.

- Healthy connections can alleviate and protect against depression.

- No matter where you are starting from, it is possible to enhance feelings of belonging.

Chapter 11

Deepening:

Renew Yourself from Within

For humankind, a growing gap between our inner selves and outer selves—an imbalance between how we live our lives and how we would like to live them—leaves the spirit thirsting for renewal.

From *Before Life Hurries By* by Sabra Field and J. Lingelbach

Kristin had just described how nearly twenty years of depression had seeped into every corner of her life—career, hobbies, friendships, loves—and especially into her own relationship with her inner self. She paused and reflected for a moment. Then tears began streaming down her cheeks as she concluded with a heartrending statement: "I am more than this…my life is more than this!"

To be sure, there was a sense of sadness and loss in her words; yet there was also an edge of defiance in her voice. Beneath the surface of her suffering, there still resided a core of strength, a well of courage, and an essence of dignity that had not been lost.

Kristin herself seemed to have forgotten that she had these qualities within her. She had lost touch with this deeper part of herself. Yet it was clear that while she had been hurt, Kristin had not been defeated by depression. She was stating an authentic truth when she said, "I am more than this."

Kristin gradually emerged from her decades-long depression. She did so by following the same pathways that you have been taking to get to this point in the workbook. Still, she was left with a strong desire to become a greater version of herself, to discover the "more" that her life could become. How could she reclaim the elements of herself that she feared were lost? How could she come through on the other side of depression with greater clarity and vitality, firmly connected to her inner reservoirs of strength, wisdom, and love?

You, too, have such reservoirs within you, just waiting to be tapped. Since they lie beneath the surface, the only way to discover and align with them is to go within. This is the pursuit of a lifetime, of course, and every spiritual tradition offers depth practices to encourage such inner growth. In this chapter we will offer you guidance on how to begin this deeply personal inward journey as you, too, emerge from depression.

BEFRIENDING YOUR DEEPER SELF

The deeper self within each of us goes by various names, such as true self, higher self, authentic self, inner voice, or simply soul. Disconnection from this vital part of you can be one of the most profoundly painful aspects of depression. It is as if you have lost your connection with the very essence of your being. Yet this connection can never truly be lost—at least not permanently.

This deep inner self, as we understand it, is constantly seeking connection. It is prodding us to be fully engaged in our lives, to know and accept both the highest and lowest aspects of ourselves, to create authentic relationships with others, to be embedded in community, to have meaningful work, to know what is truly important, to be present to that which we love, to move toward that which we long for, to experience the sacred.

It is wise to learn how to listen to this inner voice. The following exercise provides guidance on how to have a conversation with your deeper self. It is something you can do once or any time the need arises as a regular way of staying aligned with your deeper needs and desires.

If this feels unfamiliar or scary, or if you wonder, *What will I find in there?* remember the fundamental principle that has been a thread throughout this workbook: *there is more right with you than wrong with you.* You need not be afraid of what you will find in your inner landscape.

Listening to the Voice Within

We need to approach this inner voice quietly and with patience, and invite rather than summon its appearance. The fundamental requirement is simply this: *attention.* The following exercise is one way to give attention to your deeper self.

You may want to purchase a separate journal or notebook if you intend to do this often. It helps to choose one that you find beautiful or appealing. You may also want to get a special pen. You could even create a separate, soulful sitting area in your home or garden to spend your reflective time. You want to be drawn toward this practice.

Listening to Your Inner Self

- Set aside enough time to do a personal reflection (at least twenty to forty minutes). Choose a time of day when you naturally feel drawn inward and also have good energy and focus

- Begin with a few moments of silence during which you set your intention for this time. You might ask for guidance and the openness to receive it.

- Write a question in your journal; if you don't have a question yet, sit quietly while you invite a question to arise. Or you could write a general question like "What is important for me to hear today?"

- Once you have formed a question, close your eyes and hold the question lightly in your mind. You don't need to think too hard about it, because you're not trying to figure it out. Allow the thinking mind to go into the background, and see if you can let the question sink further into your being.

- Continue sitting until you feel something arise in response to your question. It may be an image, a sensation, a feeling, a color, or a sense of movement. Or it may be particular words. Again, you don't need to figure this out. Just as soon as you notice something arise, open your eyes and pick up your journal and pen.

- Just below your question, begin writing or drawing whatever comes to you. Just write, uncensored, and allow it to keep flowing out of you and through the pen as if it had a life of its own. Keep writing until you feel finished with that particular question.

- Next you may want to look at what you've written and reflect upon it, bringing your thinking mind back to the forefront. As you read and reflect, see if a new, clarifying question arises and write it down. Or you may want to write a response to what you have just read.

- If you had an additional question come up, sit with that question for a few moments until you feel another response arising, and go through the same process. Keep writing and reflecting until you feel finished for the present time.

- Look over what you have written and try to capture the essence of it: what are the kernels of wisdom, new insights or particular actions that you would like to take?

- Return to this inner dialogue as often as you'd like to stay in touch with the ground of your being.

Questions sometimes arise from this process, such as "How do I know if what I'm getting from this is real?" "What if I just made it up?" "How do I know if this inner guidance is worth following or not?" Discernment is a challenging part of the relationship with the inner life. While there are no surefire ways of validating this process, there are signs (listed in the box) that can help assure you that you are on the right track.

How to Tell If Your Inner Voice Is Authentic

- During the listening process, your thinking mind gives way to your creative mind.

- There is a sense of openness and flowing as you write.

- The words are clear and unambiguous—maybe even authoritative.

- You have a sense of resonance with it—it just *feels* true.

- The tone is supportive, affirming, and reassuring, even if it is saying difficult things that you need to hear.

- If guidance is given, there is a sense of positive, forward movement in it.

- The inner voice is always kind and loving, never harsh or critical.

- During and after the dialogue, you feel peaceful, connected, and expansive.

- You can look at it and say, "Whether this is real or not, *this* is how I'd like to live my life."

DEPRESSION AS AN OCCASION FOR AWAKENING

While the battle with depression can leave you feeling diminished, it is also possible to emerge from the encounter and be somehow enlarged by it. Depression can encourage you to listen to your inner voice.

So as you come out of depression, we urge you neither to push the experience away nor to hold on to it too tightly. There is a middle way that just might help you awaken to a larger version of yourself.

Opening to the Inner Life

Poet Anita Barrows refers to depression as a "permeable darkness" (Barrows 2006)—not something to be escaped from, but rather as an opportunity to listen, to deepen, to be "ripened" through your experience. While we do not view depression as *necessary* for deep personal growth, we do believe that you can come out on the other side with new life and greater depth.

The following exercise will invite you to look at your own experience of emergence from the darkness of depression. Please remember to be gentle with yourself, and to do this only if you feel you have enough distance from the intensity of depression that you feel ready to look into the experience without becoming caught up again in the pain of it.

After the exercise, there is an example from Kristin's own dialogue process. You may wish to read her responses first, to give you a sense of what this process can look like; or you can first write your responses if you think that would help your own voice to come forth. The choice is yours.

Guided Imagery: Emerging from Depression

Choose a quiet time and place, and give yourself at least thirty to forty-five minutes for this exercise. Have colored pens or watercolors with drawing paper at your side (or just pen and paper if you prefer to write).

- Sit quietly, eyes closed, and enjoy a few moments of awareness of your breathing. Allow your mind to settle. Then place your awareness on your heart center.

- Allow an image to arise of a garden—your garden—in the early spring. It is a time for the new, a time of hope. The garden may be in a place you know, like the garden plot in your yard now or when you were a child. Or it may be a place you imagine, one of your creating. See it now in full detail. How big is the garden? Is it surrounded by trees…hills…water? Imagine the smells, the sounds, the feel of the springtime air.

- Now imagine that you are walking through the garden to examine it. Winter has just receded, and you see the remnants of your garden's earlier life, along with the effects of the winter. Notice what you feel as you stand in the midst of this debris.

- Next, see yourself as you kneel down to get a closer look, clearing away some of the leaves and other waste from the life before winter set in. As you do so, you note that this will become valuable compost, providing essential nutrients and protection for what is soon to emerge.

- Still on your knees, you look closer underneath the debris. Then you see what you had hoped for—tender green shoots, just beginning to emerge from the dark, moist soil. You make mental notes about what it will take to nurture them along and what you need to remove in order for the new plants to flourish.

- When you're ready, pick up your drawing or writing materials. Remain in a meditative state and begin to draw (or describe) what you saw in the guided imagery. Take as much time as you need for this, letting yourself express whatever comes up without evaluating or analyzing it.

When you have finished drawing or writing, set your materials aside and hold your work in front of you. Look at it closely, not trying to figure it out but just seeing if you are drawn to any of the images, and feeling what they bring up in you. Start with a question below, or one of your own, and sit quietly until a response begins to arise. Then write until you feel finished before doing the same with another question.

Describe the experience of standing in your garden at this moment in your life, surveying the effects of a long, hard winter.

What needs to be cleared away? What is dead and of no use? What can you save and use for fertilizer or compost?

Describe the new growth beneath the muck and debris. What wants to emerge? What does it require of you in this tender stage?

How full is your garden? Is there too much, so that some needs to be thinned out in order for that which you really want to flourish? Or do you need to add more, to bring newness into it? If so, what would that be?

When you feel finished, close your eyes once more. Bring your awareness back to your heart center and notice any gratitude you have for your experience.

End with a closing ritual, if desired.

- *Kristin's Imagery*

"At first glance, my garden looks pretty barren. I feel worn out, and kind of beaten up by the winter I've been through. It's a wonder that I could survive it. That tells me something about my strength. I must be more resilient than I thought!

It feels hard to pick up the pieces of my life. I've lost so much. Still, I'm feeling better, and more hopeful now than I have for a long time. I can look at my garden and see signs of life, too.

A lot of the dead stuff in my garden seems like it came from someone else's life; it doesn't really feel like me at all. Some of the habits I picked up—lying around on weekends, keeping to myself so much, eating things I know aren't good for me—that's not me! I used to be so active; friends used to be so important to me. Now I have some relationships that just aren't healthy for me. I want to start paying more attention to how I feel when I'm with certain people.

I've made some mistakes, that's for sure, but maybe I don't have to be so hard on myself. I want to be able to grow from my 'failures' and to remember that I'm always doing the best that I can at that moment. For example, I think there's a disconnect between me and my job. Work is not a healthy place for me right now—too much pressure and people are too negative. I'm ready for something new.

I've always been so busy; that was probably one of the reasons I'd get depressed, because I was so stressed. Now, though, my garden looks a little sparse. I want to add things without overdoing it. I think the two things most important to add right now are really quality friends—and playing more. I want to learn how to be a good friend and to have more fun again!

I'm also excited about getting to know myself better, to spend more time reflecting or just being quiet. I didn't think that was really important, but now I see myself differently. I'm someone worth knowing."

Becoming Your Authentic Self

A friend was spending time with his family, when a song reminded him of his adolescent dream of becoming a rock star. Specifically, he had wanted to be Bob Dylan. Upon hearing this, his four-year-old niece pointedly remarked, "Uncle Larry, you can only be who you really are!"

To live with joy, it is important that you become who you really are. That sounds so simple—how could you be anything but yourself? Yet many people are really trying to be someone else, a choice that can create unhappiness no matter how good the other person seems to be, because it is not authentic for you.

Dawna Markova writes: "Healing insists that you reexamine everything—all of your habits, ideas, beliefs, values, passions, inhibitions, assumptions—until you find those things that are truest at the core, discarding everything else. It demands that you nurture your questions until you discover how to create the kind of environment where you have integrity with yourself and the world on a daily basis" (Markova 1994, 12).

If that sounds like hard work, it is. But it is also one of life's primary purposes and can become a source of great joy. One of your greatest aids in the search to become yourself is to move toward that which you deeply desire.

Picture a swan walking toward its desire: a calm pond on a hot summer's day. That's the image in a well-known poem called "The Swan" (Rilke 1982, 29). The poet, Rilke, describes a swan moving clumsily on land, as if his legs were caught up in ropes. Haven't we all had times of moving awkwardly through our days with great effort, held back from success or happiness as if we, too, were bound by ropes?

But the swan just keeps moving toward the water, as if he is irresistibly drawn toward it. And then, when he reaches the water, all awkwardness dissolves as he is held effortlessly and moves gracefully, looking like a king in complete control of his destiny. He has found his element.

It is easy to become focused on the struggle, on the things that seem to hold you back. But in Rilke's poem, the swan doesn't bother too much with that. He doesn't try to understand or fix his problems, doesn't need to separate them one by one, or name them or get rid of them. He doesn't look outside himself for reasons for "what's wrong." Instead, he just lumbers on, unconcerned about his awkwardness, until he reaches the water's edge and is transformed.

Suddenly, there are no more ropes, no more things left undone, no more awkwardness. When you find your water—your true home—and enter it, the poet says that moment is a little bit like dying. In order to leave the familiar ground on which you have been standing, you have to let go of the life that you have clung to so very tightly. You must let go of the old, the firmness of what is known, to make room for the new.

Once upon the water, the awkward bird is transformed into a thing of beauty and majesty, effortlessly gliding ahead toward an unknown future. Despite the uncertainty into which it moves, the swan is at total peace, completely at home.

It can be like that for you, too. When you finally enter your element, when you let go of the striving, when you stop trying to be good or to get something that will fill you up, then you, too, can float effortlessly upon your own life. You can let yourself be guided by your life stream, neither pushing against the current nor grasping at the banks. Of course, you will still face pain, failure, and loss—as we have seen, they are part of the condition of life. But if what you want is joy, then you can stop fighting the flow of life. You can surrender to your life, becoming more and more fully yourself.

Finding Your Element

Ask yourself these questions, allowing yourself time to reflect on them. Notice whatever comes up for you: images, memories, ideas, feelings. You may want to use the dialogue process described previously:

What is your water? What is your element? When do you feel most at home?

What are you like when you feel most alive?

When and where do you come alive like this? Who are you with, what are the activities, what are the conditions that bring you to life, that give you the greatest joy?

THE SOUL WAS MEANT FOR JOY

This workbook began with the statement "Surely joy is the condition of life." Hard as it is to believe that sentiment at times, we have come to see the deep truth in Thoreau's words. Joy is present at all times, providing an undercurrent of sustenance and support, whether or not we realize it is there.

Many people long for a dramatic spiritual awakening—some sort of out-of-body or mountaintop experience—in the hopes that it will be life changing and finally, once and for all, open them to joy. But there are many ways to awaken, and other, subtler paths that can lead to a more sustained experience of joy.

Charlotte Joko Beck, a pioneering Zen teacher, once said, "Joy is exactly what's happening, minus our opinion of it" (Beck 1994, 233). In other words, it is simpler than we think—not easy, but simple—to access joy, because it can be present in anything.

Here is how one traveler of these pathways described a recent experience of joy:

I had had a difficult day, and I was struggling with my mood. I'd already worked all day and had to work that evening, but I took a little break and went for a walk along a busy bike path. For the first few minutes, I became absorbed in my thoughts, focused upon all that was going wrong. But then I noticed that my mood was low, so I decided to put what I had learned to the test. I placed my awareness on my heart, inviting it to open as best it could. Then, whenever someone passed by on foot or on bicycle, I silently offered a blessing as I held my heart open to that person.

If they seemed preoccupied or low, I said to myself, May you be at peace. I wish you well. If they seemed happy or smiling, I said, I'm so glad that you are happy. Your joy is my joy.

I went along like this, but in a few minutes something had changed. People began to notice me and look over at me. Soon, more and more of the passersby were smiling—at me! As I continued, my heart opened further, and I felt lighter myself.

For about an hour after that, it felt like everything was just as it should be, that everything was going to be all right. I felt like I belonged, like I could go up to anyone and I would be accepted, just as I am. I know an hour doesn't seem like much, but it filled me with hope. It reminded me of what life could be like. And the really great thing is that I was present for it. I was really there, so I could enjoy it. I would even say I felt joyful. So now the experience is etched in my mind. It tells me that joy is really possible—even for me!

Throughout all the pathways to joy, we have been encouraging you to discover for yourself what obstacles might prevent you from accessing your own experience of joy. You have looked at all the body pathways that must be addressed, yet are not usually sufficient by themselves to open to joy. You have worked with the mind pathways, seeking to awaken more fully to your life in the present moment. But what is it you want to awaken into? What kind of world, what kind of life, is worth awakening for? Those are questions, we believe, that can only be answered by the heart.

The one thing that you can always do is to be completely present. Be fully present to your life as it is, and you will find joy, at least occasionally. You may still choose to revisit any of the nine pathways in this workbook to further open your access to joy—and when you do, be assured that it will be there. Whenever and wherever you do find joy, be sure to notice it, drink it in, and celebrate it.

SUMMING UP CHAPTER 11

- There is within you a larger self, and it is wise to give it your attention.

- Emerging from depression can be a time of awakening, of coming more fully to life.

- Listening within, you can be guided by what you most long for, by what brings authentic joy.

References

Akhondzadeh S., H. R. Naghavi, M. Vazirian, A. Shayeganpour, H. Rashidi, and M. Khani. 2001. Passionflower in the treatment of generalized anxiety: A pilot double-blind randomized controlled trial with oxazepam. *Journal of Clinical Pharmacy and Therapeutics* 26: 363–67.

Albarracin C., B. Fuqua, J. L. Evans, and I. D. Goldfine. 2008. Chromium picolinate and biotin combination improves glucose metabolism in treated, uncontrolled overweight to obese patients with type 2 diabetes. *Diabetes Metabolism Research and Reviews* 24: 41–51.

Alpert J. E., G. Papakostas, D. Mischoulon, J. J. Worthington III, T. Petersen, and Y. Mahal. 2004. S-Adenosyl-L-methionine (SAMe) as an adjunct for resistant major depressive disorder: An open trial following partial or nonresponse to selective serotonin reuptake inhibitors or venlafaxine. *Journal of Clinical Psychopharmacology* 24: 661–64.

Barrows, A. 2006. "The Soul in Depression." Speaking of Faith. American Public Media. MPR. November 16, 2006.

Beck, C. 1994. *Nothing Special: Living Zen*. New York: Harper One.

Berk, M., D. L. Copolov, O. Dean, K. Lu, S. Jeavons, I. Schapkaitz, M. Anderson-Hunt, and A. I. Bush. 2008. N-acetyl cysteine for depressive symptoms in bipolar disorder: A double-blind randomized placebo-controlled trial. *Biological Psychiatry* 64 (6): 468–75.

Bray, G. A., S. J. Nielson, and B. M. Popkin. 2004. Consumption of high-fructose corn syrup in beverages may play a role in the epidemic of obesity. *American Journal of Clinical Nutrition* 79 (4): 537–43.

Calaprice, A. 2005. *The New Quotable Einstein.* Princeton, NJ: Princeton University Press.

Chadwick, D. 2007. *Zen is Right Here: Teaching Stories and Anecdotes of Shunryu Suzuki.* Boston, MA: Shambhala Publications.

Davidson, J. R., K. Abraham, K. M. Connor, and M. N. McLeod. 2003. Effectiveness of chromium in atypical depression: A placebo-controlled trial. *Biological Psychiatry* 53 (3): 261–26.

Davidson J. R., and the Hypericum Depression Trial Study Group. 2002. Effect of Hypericum perforatum (St. John's wort) in major depressive disorder: A randomized controlled trial. *Journal of the American Medical Association* 287: 1807–14.

Dusek, J. A., C. Denton, H. Emmons, L. Knutson, S. Masemer, and G. Plotnikoff. 2009. Evaluation of an 8-week resilience training program in moderate to severely depressed patients. *Explore: The Journal of Science and Healing* 5 (3): 160–1.

Fredrickson, B. L., K. A. Coffey, and J. Pek. 2008. Open hearts build lives: Positive emotions, induced through loving-kindness meditation, build consequential personal resources. *Journal of Personality and Social Psychology* 95 (5): 1045–62.

Glozier, N., A. Martiniuk, G. Patton, R. Ivers, Q. Li, I. Hickie, T. Senserrick, M. Woodward, R. Norton, and M. Stevenson. 2010. Short sleep duration in prevalent and persistent psychological distress in young adults: The DRIVE Study. *Sleep* 33 (9): 1139–45.

Goleman, D. 1995. *Emotional Intelligence: Why It Can Matter More than IQ.* New York, NY: Bantam Books.

Holt-Lunstad, J., T. B. Smith, and J. B. Layton. 2010. Social relationships and mortality risk: A meta-analysis review. *PLoS Medicine* 7 (7): 1–9.

Kessler, R. C., W. T. Chiu, O. Demler, and E. E. Walters. 2005. Prevalence, severity, and comorbidity of twelve-month DSM-IV disorders in the National Comorbidity Survey Replication (NCS-R). *Archives of General Psychiatry* 62 (6): 617–27.

Kilpatrick, L. A., B. Y. Suyenobu, S. R. Smith, J. A. Bueller, T. Goodman, J. D. Creswell, K. Tillisch, E. A. Mayer, and B. D. Naliboff. 2011. Impact of mindfulness-based stress reduction training on intrinsic brain connectivity. *Neuroimage* 56 (1): 290–8.

Knauper, B., A. McCollam, A. Rosen-Brown, J. Lacaille, E. Kelso, and M. Roseman. 2011. Fruitful plans: Adding targeted mental imagery to implementation intentions increases fruit consumption. *Psychology and Health* 18: 1–17.

Kross, E., M. G. Berman, W. Mischel, E. E. Smith, and T. D. Wagner. 2011. Social rejection shares somatosensary representation with physical pain. *Proceedings of the National Academy of Sciences* 108 (15): 6270–75.

Lakhan, S. E., and K. F. Vieira. 2008. Nutritional therapies for mental disorders: Review. *Nutrition Journal* 7: 2. doi:10.1186/1475-2891-7-2.

Linde, K., M. M. Berner, and L. Kriston. 2009. St. John's wort for major depression. *Cochrane Library of Systematic Reviews*, Issue 4.

Luders, E., A. W. Toga, N. Lepore, and C. Gaser. 2009. The underlying anatomical correlates of long-term meditation: Larger hippocampal and frontal volumes of gray matter. *Neuroimage* 45 (3): 672–78.

Maes, M., M. Kubera, and J. C. Leunis. 2008. The gut-brain barrier in major depression: Intestinal mucosal dysfunction with an increased translocation of LPS from gram negative enterobacteria (leaky gut) plays a role in the pathophysiology of depression. *Neuroendocrinology Letters* 29 (1): 117–24.

Markova, D. 1994. *No Enemies Within*. Newburyport, MA: Conari Press.

Miller, A. H., V. Maletic, and C. L. Raison. 2010. Inflammation and its discontents: The role of cytokines in the pathophysiology of major depression. *Biological Psychiatry* 65(9): 732–41.

Mota-Pereira, J., J. Silverio, S. Caevalho, J. C. Riberio, D. Fonte, and J. Ramos. 2011. Moderate exercise improves depression parameters in treatment-resistant patients with major depressive disorder. *Psychiatry Research* 45 (8): 1005–11.

Nadia I., E. D. Dalton, M. Fava, and D. Mischoulon. 2011. Second-tier natural antidepressants: Review and critique. *Journal of Affective Disorders* 130 (3): 343–57.

Nathan P. J., K. Lu, M. Gray, and C. Oliver. 2006. The neuropharmacology of L-theanine. *Journal of Herbal Pharmacotherapy* 6 (2): 21–30.

Nettleton, J. A., P. L. Lutsey, Y. Wang, J. A. Lima, E. D. Michos, and D. R. Jacobs. 2009. Diet soda intake and risk of incident metabolic syndrome and type 2 diabetes in the Multi-Ethnic Study of Atherosclerosis (MESA). *Diabetes Care* 32 (4): 688–94.

Nouwen, H. 1994. *Here and Now*. New York, NY: Crossroad Publishing.

O'Keefe, J. H., M. N. Geewala, and J. O. O'Keefe. 2008. Dietary strategies for improving postprandial glucose lipids, inflammation, and cardiovascular disease. *Journal of the American College of Cardiology* 51 (3): 249–55.

Oyle, I. 1979. The New American Medicine Show. Santa Cruz, CA. Unity Press.

Qin, B., K. S. Panickar, and R. A. Anderson. 2010. Cinnamon: Potential role in the prevention of insulin resistance, metabolic syndrome and type 2 diabetes. *Journal of Diabetes Science and Technology* 4 (3): 685–93.

Rilke, R. 1982. *The Selected Poetry of Rainer Maria Rilke* (Trans. by Stephen Michell). New York: Random House.

Ruhé, H. G., N. S. Mason, and A. H. Schene. 2007. Mood is indirectly related to serotonin, norepinephrine and dopamine levels in humans: A meta-analysis of monoamine depletion studies. *Molecular Psychiatry* 12 (4): 331–59.

Shute, N. 2011. Antidepressant use climbs, as primary care doctors do the prescribing. *Shots*, National Public Radio, www.npr.org/blogs/health/2011/08/06/138987152/antidepressant-use-climbs-as-primary-care-doctors-do-the-prescribing.

Silber, B., and J. Schmitt. 2010. Effects of tryptophan loading on human cognition, mood and sleep. *Neuroscience and Biobehavioral Reviews* 34 (3): 387–407.

Smith, K. W. 2011. Depression: A repair response to stress-induced neuronal microdamage that can grade into a chronic neuroinflammatory condition? *Neuroscience and Behavioral Reviews* 35 (30): 742–64.

Strasser, A., M. Skalicky, M. Hansalik, and A. Viidik. 2006. The impact of environment in comparison with moderate physical exercise and dietary restriction on BDNF in the cerebral parietotemporal cortex of aged Sprague-Dawley rats. *Gerontology* 52 (6): 377–81.

U.S. Census Bureau. 2005. Population estimates by demographic characteristics. Table 2: Annual estimates of the population by selected age groups and sex for the United States: April 1, 2000 to July 1, 2004 (NC-EST2004-02). www.census.gov/popest/national/asrh/.

Whitman, W. 2004. "Song of the Open Road." *Leaves of Grass*. New York, NY: Bantam Dell Division of Random House.

Williams, A. L., C. Girard, D. Jui, A. Sabina, and D. L. Katz. 2005. S-Adenosylmethionine (SAMe) as treatment for depression: A systematic review. *Clinical and Investigative Medicine* 28: 132–9.

World Health Organization. 2008. *The global burden of disease: 2004 update*. Table A2: Burden of disease in DALYs by cause, sex and income group in WHO regions, estimates for 2004. Geneva, Switzerland: World Health Organization. http://www.who.int/healthinfo/global_burden_disease/GBD_report_2004update_AnnexA.pdf.

Henry Emmons, MD, is a psychiatrist who integrates mind-body and natural therapies, mindfulness, and compassionate insight into his clinical work. He developed and runs the resilience training program offered at the Penny George Institute for Health and Healing in Minneapolis, MN. He is author of *The Chemistry of Joy* and *The Chemistry of Calm*. www.partnersinresilience.com

Susan Bourgerie, MA, LP, is an experienced psychotherapist and cofounder of Loring Psychotherapy and Mindfulness Center in Minneapolis, MN. She is part of the team delivering the resilience training program offered at the Penny George Institute for Health and Healing.

Carolyn Denton, MA, LN, is an integrative nutritionist who focuses not only on general health and disease prevention, but also nutrition as a complementary therapy for chronic and degenerative diseases. She is a member of the integrative medicine team at the Penny George Institute for Health and Healing.

Sandra Kacher, MSW, LICSW, has over twenty-five years of clinical experience and is cofounder of Loring Psychotherapy and Mindfulness Center. She is a founding team member of the resilience training program at the Penny George Institute for Health and Healing.

Index

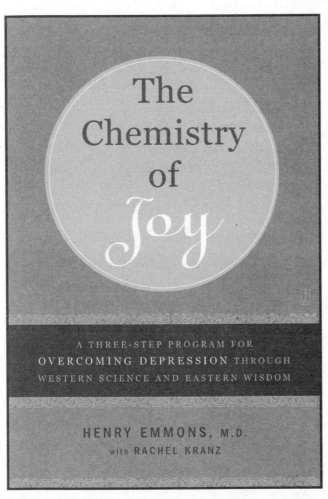